This book is dedicated to all those people who keep 'em flying.

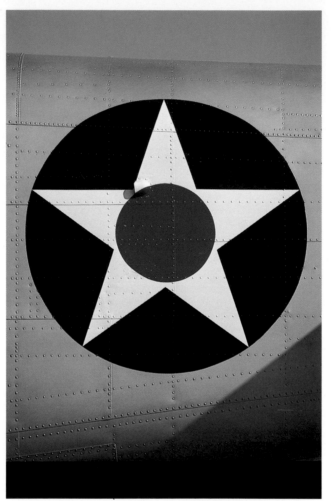

Designed by Marilyn F. Appleby
Edited by Ross A. Howell, Jr., and Kathleen D. Valenzi,
with the assistance of Karen M. Cauthen, Carlotta M. Eike,
Joan Berry Horen, and Gina M. Wallace.
Photography copyright © 1987 by Mark Meyer. All rights reserved.
Introduction copyright © 1987 by Walter J. Boyne. All rights reserved.
This book, or any portions thereof, may not be reproduced
or transmitted in any form or by any means, electronic or mechanical,
including photocopying, recording, or by any information storage and
retrieval system, without permission in writing from the publisher.
The introduction may not be reproduced without permission of Walter J. Boyne.
Library of Congress Catalog Card Number 87-80777
ISBN 0-943231-41-8
Manufactured in Hong Kong.
Published by Howell Press, Inc., 1147 River Road, Bay 2,
Charlottesville, Virginia 22901. Telephone (804) 977-4006.
Sixth printing

HOWELL PRESS

CLASSICS

U.S. AIRCRAFT OF WORLD WAR II

PHOTOGRAPHY BY MARK MEYER

INTRODUCTION BY WALTER J. BOYNE

Is there a rational explanation for grown men and women spending thousands of dollars and the best years of their lives coaxing 40-year-old airplanes back into the air? If you are romantic, if your heart beats faster when *The Star Spangled Banner* is played, if you like old movies and old cars, then you know that there are many explanations. It would be flip, however, to dismiss the booming interest in classics as mere patriotism and nostalgia when there are far more meaningful psychological, aesthetic, and engineering reasons. These glamorous veterans tell us much about ourselves as they slip through the sky in evocation of the past.

Yet patriotism and nostalgia are certainly important. Some wars just seem better than others. None are good while they are in progress, but after the passage of time, the public begins to take a fancy to certain of them. The Revolutionary War and the War of 1812 never seemed to take hold, nor did the Mexican or Spanish-American wars. The Civil War, the most terrible conflict experienced by the United States in terms of casualties, gained an almost immediate affection, so much so that the names of Confederate generals soon graced military posts of the very nation they had fought against. The first World War was simply too horrible to capture people's imaginations, although the flyers of that war have been glamorized to some degree. The Korean War has been forgotten, and we are just witnessing the beginning of popular interest in the terrible experience of Viet Nam.

But, ah,...World War II, a vintage war with memories for everyone. Americans shared an absolute gut-feeling that it was a good war, that we were the good guys. Our enemies were demonstrably, irrevocably evil, and their defeat was sure to be welcomed, even by their own people.

It was not only that we were fighting for the right cause; the war changed the country, pulling it laughing and proud from the depths of a major depression. It showed us strengths we didn't know that we had, developing the economy so that our influence extended throughout the world. And the most obvious symbols of this enormous change were our Army, Navy, and Marine air forces. Who would forget that airpower bombed us into the war on December 7, 1941, or that it bombed our way out in 1945?

Our engineering achievements were phenomenal. In 1939 aviation was a cottage industry in the United States, building a few thousand relatively simple airplanes annually. By 1941 we had enough warning to develop a wider base, but we were still naive when it came to war-making, producing airplanes with armor, armament, and equipment not greatly different from those used in 1918. Production levels seemed impossibly high compared to the past, but it was just the beginning. Not only would vastly more aircraft be produced (300,000 airplanes delivered—at a cost of $45 billion), but they were far more complex. The war had begun with the bombing of Pearl Harbor and with lovely, but impotent, Martin B-10s and Boeing P-26s being blown to pieces at Clark Field. It ended less than four years later with Boeing B-29 Superfortress bombers and North American P-51 Mustang fighters ranging over the heart of Japan, unable to find targets worth destroying.

Certainly, the major reason for the resurgent interest in classics is their sheer aesthetic appeal. These lovely fighter and bomber aircraft, from Hellcat to Marauder, from Jug to Liberator, from Corsair to Texan, have a unique quality not found elsewhere in the world of art. Absolutely beautiful sculptures at rest, they transform themselves into transcendental, kinetic masterpieces in flight. This is the change which stirs our souls, and this is what Mark Meyer has captured on film. The alteration is elusive; thousands of photographs of aircraft are just that—pictures of planes. To capture the inner beauty, the photographer must be in resonance with the subject in order to frame with his lens the airframe's latent beauty.

The transformation Meyer seeks begins with soft buzzes and clicks as electrical power is connected. It builds with a mechanical banging as control surfaces are checked, hatches are opened and closed, and commands are shouted from pilot to ground. The whining starter is drowned out by the rise and fall of random explosions merging into coughs of blue-white smoke as the engine rumbles to life. Shouted commands can no longer be heard—hand signals cause the chocks to be pulled, and the airplane lurches forward, still not fully formed, still ground-bound. Not until after the takeoff, when the gear and flaps are up, when the power roars, not to overcome the friction of earth but to summon flight from the sky, is the change complete.

And it is in the air that art and metal truly merge. On the ground the aerodynamic forces tug in one direction only—to the ground. In flight there are infinite vectors of direction. Lift sucks upward, not only at the cambered wings, but on the fuselage as well. It pulls both up and down on the tail, giving variations on its own theme. The airplane seems to duck to shed drag, to rid itself of the encumbrances to flight. The thrust pours back from the engine and propellers, swirling streamlines of moisture to mix with thin trails of exhaust smoke.

And there is still, and always, gravity, overcome in level flight by the other members of the famous lift/drag/thrust/weight equation, but reimposed in doubled or tripled terms with every steep turn. The induced "gravitational" change, known as g force, is evident on a human body inside the aircraft; outside, its subtle evidence can be fixed only by a photographer in tune with his subject, who can collect on film the invisible forces that raise airframe to artwork.

It's a miracle that any are left to see. America proved that it could demobilize even faster than it mobilized, and thousands of aircraft were disposed of brutally. Some spent months or years baking in the desert sun before being cut up to become pots and pans; others were simply crumpled

by bulldozers and dumped into land fill. It was not only the return to peace that caused the wastage; the debut of the jet engine seemed to render any World War II airplane obsolete.

Yet some lingered on. The Learjet and its brethren were still in the future, so many companies converted Douglas Invaders, Martin Marauders, and North American Mitchells purchased from war surplus stocks at bargain-basement prices into executive planes. They were expensive to operate, but they were the fastest things around, and for many they exemplified a time that would never come again. The racing community naturally embraced the fighters, never dreaming that the hot new unlimiteds of 1947 would be the hot old unlimiteds of 1987. Many of the famous transport warbirds—C-46s, C-47s, C-54s—went either to civil work or to smaller wars. And then there were the sentimentalists, people who just liked the airplane they flew—or didn't get to fly—and who couldn't resist buying their love object at giveaway prices.

Thus it is that we can enjoy whole formations of immaculate Mustangs more than four decades after test pilot Vance Breese took the first North American NA-73X from Mines Field in 1940. Other types are in shorter supply. There are only a handful of Wildcat, Hellcat, and Thunderbolt fighters still flying. As the cost of operation goes up, the number of aircraft operating goes down. Only one B-29 Superfortress bomber, the fabulous Fifi, stays in the air. A Martin Marauder bomber, lovingly restored by the Confederate Air Force, was airborne for a while, and will be again. There are enough B-25 Mitchell bombers and two-engined Catalinas, flying boats once used for bombing and rescue, to last us, and a comparative surplus of Gooney Bird transports.

Perhaps the only thing of which you can be sure, however, is that you can't be sure of anything. Twenty years ago, no one would have believed that restorers could reach deep into the New Guinea jungles and bring forth Japanese fighters to fly again. Who would have thought that four Halberstadt ground-attack planes from World War I would survive in the attic of a German town hall until the 1970s, complete with spare engines, fitted and lined tool kits, yards of camouflage fabric, handbooks—the time capsule of a squadron repair shop? And then there are the grandiose projects, like the rescue of four Lockheed P-38 Lightnings and the odd B-17 Flying Fortress immured in 40 feet of snow in Greenland for four decades. Never say never. There were no German Daimler-Benz-engined Messerschmitt Bf 109 fighters flying anywhere in the years after the war, nor any French Dewoitine D 520 fighters. Suddenly, one of each was flying in its native country. Sadly, just as suddenly, both were totally destroyed in accidents. Of this, more later.

Undoubtedly part of the lure of these machines is the satisfaction of transforming a battered and rusted hulk into an accurately, painstakingly restored showpiece. The restorer experiences a sense of fulfillment at locating a neglected warbird and cleverly procuring it at the lowest possible price (possibly for only a mortgage on your house). There are some difficulties on the way, beginning with the back-breaking labor of hauling it from its resting place on a flatbed truck to a hangar whose rent seems to go up monthly. It is in this process that one finds that a disassembled aircraft handles nothing like an assembled one; there are no pick-up points to facilitate any necessary rigging, no known centers of gravity to help determine points of balance. A fighter fuselage with engine installed is a wild and fractious thing, with a headstrong center of gravity so far forward that it sheds ropes and tag lines and threatens to tip forklifts over. These are the troubles that are considered fun in retrospect, made easier by the knowledge that you have a nascent classic. The picture of the future, when the tired shards are transformed into something spectacular, is

enough to keep you going. If it doesn't have an engine, or tires, or landing gear, there is always Trade-A-Plane, and it's only money.

Oddly enough, engines and tires and landing gears will not be the major problem. The real difficulties come in getting the hydraulic accumulators, the bomb racks, the thousand other bits that make up the equipment list. The time-consuming and arduous process is punctuated by sudden finds and by abject disappointments. The long-sought generator, supposedly unavailable anywhere, materializes at an airport a mere 800 miles away. After a quick flight over and the money changes hands (it's *only* money, remember), you find that it won't fit because your warbird was modified. But there are other kinds of luck as well; nowhere in the world is the radiator you need—except by chance in the garage down the street, in the box, mint, and cheap.

It is a process familiar to automobile collectors, but much more rarified. For as the hulk slowly changes, as the rust disappears and the parts come together, the restorer becomes ever more conscious that this bird is going to fly, and that the parts can't just look right—they have to *be* right.

Restoration calls for all the elements of backyard, shade-tree, mechanical genius to be combined with the evaluative eye of a surgeon. Can a piston be swapped from one engine to another? How much of the metal will have to be replaced when the reskinning starts? Will you be able to use synthetic materials in the seals? These questions take on added significance when you consider the amount of careful scrutiny your aircraft will undergo once restoration is complete. When you are finished, the layman will admire the airplane extravagantly, but there are experts lurking out there who will not hesitate to point out that Technical Order 1894478, a military document dated 3 August 1943, moved the fuel stencil eight inches to the left of where you have it. If you have to strip the paint and repaint it to move the stencil, well, that's the price of perfection. In this case, money isn't the issue—it's a matter of honor.

Even though it seems a distant thing for most of the restoration, the question of flying the aircraft is always uppermost in your mind. Why worry about flying when you cannot find an intake manifold, a control run, or a starter motor? But as each of these is located, the thrill is allayed by the nagging realization that you are one step closer to first flight day.

There are a number of attitudes that can be adopted at this point, ranging from the stupid to the cowardly, and cowardly is best. On the one hand, you can reason, "Well, I've got two hundred hours in a Comanche, so I'll take six hours in the back seat of a T-6 trainer and then test this single-engine Corsair fighter myself. I just won't make any sudden power applications." Or you can say, "I'll find a pilot current in the airplane, offer him a fee to test-fly this bent-wing dude for me, pay his expenses,..." and live a lot longer.

It doesn't have to be a fighter plane to bite you, either. Even a newly restored T-6 can be a handful to a Piper Cub pilot, and any multi-engine airplane has the strong possibility of engine-out operation.

The passage of 40 years has not made the elegant classic aircraft any less an example of engineering prowess. These warbirds were not designed as toys for weekend flying, but rather as killing machines, or as machines to train people for killing machines. For many restorers, being familiar with a particular line of aircraft and establishing a close, hands-on relationship during the process of rebuilding tends to mask the truth of the plane's sophistication. The argument "I'll be flying it light" is often made as a reason to discount the demanding characteristics of a warplane. This argument is true in part. A P-47 "Jug" Thunderbolt at a maximum gross weight of 15,000 pounds, laden with eight machine guns, 3,400 rounds of ammunition, a 200-gallon external tank, rockets and bombs, and operating from a grass field is far different from your stripped-down Jug weighing in at 11,000 pounds lifting off from a concrete airstrip. The lighter weight is offset by quicker acceleration, which means that the powerful torque will get at you that much sooner. Plus you have 40-year-old systems—oil coolers, intercoolers, whatever—all of which can get you into deep trouble.

The question of pilot proficiency is double-edged, as well, for a great deal of flight time can be as hazardous as too little. To use a pop-psychology cliche—what one needs is "quality time." During the war, young pilots were brought along in hectic procession on trainers like the PT-17s, BT-13s, and AT-6s. From there they may have moved on to the P-40 Warhawk single-engine fighter before receiving instruction on other types of almost new airplanes. Their flying experience was intense, recent, and closely supervised. Even today's 50-year-old airline pilot, veteran of 25,000 hours (22,000 on the autopilot) does not have the level of consciousness needed to handle a hot, 40-year-old fighter.

The previously mentioned Messerschmitt and Dewoitine crashes are perfect examples. Both aircraft were carefully and professionally restored with no expense spared and with the resources of their respective national air forces behind them. Both were flown by highly experienced jet test pilots. In the case of the Messerschmitt, it was destroyed in an accident representative of the kind that occurred so often during the war. The pilot lost control on takeoff, and the beautifully restored "Gustav," its Daimler-Benz engine sonorously pouring forth power, impacted in a parking lot full of cars. As for the test pilot of the Dewoitine D 520, he was well aware of the hot little fighter's tendency to flick-roll if too much back pressure was applied, because veterans had told him that at certain airspeeds and g forces, just a hint of pressure on the stick could send it rolling. He was only unaware of how *little* pressure and how *fast* the roll, and in this case, the airplane flick-rolled him into the ground.

The primary cause of both accidents was the pilot's

lack of experience in handling one of the airplane's peculiarities, the result of inevitable compromises by which the designers achieved performance at the cost of docile handling. Nothing in the training of the two test pilots, even their awareness of the hazards, could have prepared them to react in time to avoid an accident. So what chance does the pilot of a small, private plane like the Bonanza have?

Well, pretty good—if he is extraordinarily careful at all times, if he trains himself carefully, and if his maintenance practices are superb. After learning the hard way, the Confederate Air Force, which has done so much to keep the classic airplanes flying, developed a rigorous program to make the flying safe. There is certainly no easy way, no off-hand way, and no inexpensive way to learn to fly these aircraft properly.

This isn't fate, or bureaucracy, or anything else we normally blame things on. It is the direct result of the very thing that contributed to the beauty of the classics—their strong engineering heritage. When you look at a B-17, you are seeing more than crafted metal. The genius of dozens of men and women, poured out over many years in various airplanes and engines, all comes together in this proud Fortress. What you see is the entrepreneurial daring of William Boeing, who stood willing time and again to risk his total assets on the skill of his engineers. It embodies the vision of Claire Egtvedt, who chose to interpret the "multi-engine" Army specification as meaning four engines instead of the two the Air Corps had in mind. Boeing engineers had already labored over the Monomail and B-9 prototypes, and had won no contracts. They had fashioned the revolutionary 247 transport, only to see Douglas sweep the board with its DC series. Think of the courage required of management to persist in building big, multi-engine bombers when Boeing was already well established in the fighter field with the P-26. Stockholders were as demanding then as now, so it took incredible courage for 24-year-old Ed

Wells to undertake as assistant project engineer, the super-secret Model 299 which became the Fortress.

The engines which powered the Fortress—Pratt & Whitney R-1690Es on the prototype and Wright R-1820s on the production aircraft—were themselves the result of industrial daring, genius, and years of sweat. Charles Lawrance, creator of the basic layout for the modern radial engine, had started the process. Frederick B. Rentschler brought it along, first at Wright, then later at Pratt & Whitney, where he created a new line of air-cooled radial engines. Both Lawrance and Rentschler were backed by foresighted military men who took chances with their careers and with government money to support their efforts—like Commander Jerome C. Hunsaker, who gambled on Lawrance, and Rear Admiral William A. Moffett, who supported both Wright and Pratt & Whitney at considerable risk.

The superchargers that Dr. Sanford Moss, a grey-bearded patrician, began working on for General Electric in 1918 were a similar product of toil, brains, and love. Altitude records were being set with the supercharger, a device that forced air into the combustion process of an airplane, by the early 1920s, but it took years of experimentation and improvement in the metals used on turbine wheels before the supercharger was capable of the wide use it received in WWII. Neither the B-24 nor the B-17 bombers could have made it over Germany at safe, high altitudes without it. In the process of its development, forgotten men like George A. Hallet, Opie Chenoweth, Ernest T. Jones, and C. Fayette Taylor contributed their invaluable knowledge and expertise to the project.

Thunderbolt, the rugged Republic P-47 single-engine fighter, has a similar heroic ancestry, this time stemming in large part from immigrant Russians. Alexander P. de Seversky, whose father had been the first man to own and fly an airplane in Russia, was infused with a love of flying himself, so he entered the Imperial Russian Naval Air Service in 1914. Shot down and severely injured, de Seversky lost his right leg as a result of the accident. But this did not diminish his love for flight; in fact, it barely slowed him down, because as soon as he was able, he returned to combat and became a 13-victory ace. Sent to the United States by his government, de Seversky elected to stay when he learned that the Bolsheviks had taken over his homeland. While in the States, this inventive genius sold 364 patents to the U.S. government and established his own firm, the Seversky Aircraft Corporation. One of his first products—aircraft skis with an innovative shock-absorber system that he would use again later to good advantage—seemed a natural one for a Russian inventor.

Another Russian, Alexander Kartveli, fled the Russian revolution by going to France, where in 1927 he met the flamboyant Charles Levine. Levine, Clarence Chamberlin's backer and "co-pilot" on the famous flight of the Bellanca "Columbia," established a small aircraft manufacturing business where Kartveli designed two airplane prototypes, the "Uncle Sam" and the "Triad." Neither was successful, largely because of Levine's interference. When de Seversky opened the Seversky Aircraft Corporation, he hired fellow countryman Kartveli away from Levine and made him assistant chief engineer. Ironically, the Russian revolution was a great boon to U.S. aviation, sending us Igor Sikorsky and vast numbers of skilled craftsmen, as well as de Seversky and Kartveli.

Kartveli's first design for Seversky, the SEV-3, was a three-seat floatplane that set records and clearly forecast the form the Thunderbolt would take. It was radial-engined, all metal, with a round fuselage and elegant, elliptical wings. The Kartveli touch which would become so famous—smoothly rounded surfaces, generous fillets, the appearance of raw power—was evident in the SEV-3.

Seversky and Kartveli both believed in intensive development of their basic airplane, and there followed a succession of evolutionary designs which led from the BT-8 trainer, notorious for ground looping, through the P-35, which won an order for 77 aircraft in 1936 and which was the predecessor of the P-47.

Major de Seversky was a talented engineer, pilot, and showman, but he was not the best businessman in the world, and Seversky Aircraft Corporation had to be reorganized as the Republic Aircraft Corporation. De Seversky was out, but Kartveli remained and extended his formula through XP-41 and XP-43 variations, prototypes to the P-47. At the time he was almost alone in America in selecting radial engines for Army Air Force fighters.

The big breakthrough for Kartveli came with the introduction of the enormous Pratt & Whitney R-2800 engine. It was the perfect marriage of airframe and engine heritage, the latter carrying with it the contributions of Sanford Moss. The P-47 emerged as the biggest single-place fighter ever built—a brawling bruiser capable of taking enormous punishment and coming back home. Given that 15,683 were built, it is tragic that so few survive today.

The P-47's younger and generally more popular rival, the North American P-51 Mustang, was produced by a "new" company with an even richer development history. There was a heavy Teutonic influence on the P-51, and not because the head of the company, West Virginian James Howard Kindelberger, was known as "Dutch." The Teutonic influence comes, in part, from one of the principal contributors to the P-51's design, German-born Edgar Schmued. Don Berlin, father of both the P-40 fighter and the XP-46 prototype, was also an important factor. But there probably wouldn't have been any aircraft from the firm if it hadn't been for a real Dutchman, Tony Fokker. Fokker founded the Atlantic Aircraft Corporation in May 1924, and the company became, over time and via a convoluted family tree, North American Aviation. This family tree included Curtiss Aeroplane and Motor Company, Douglas Aircraft,

General Motors, American Dornier, Berliner/Joyce, Sherman Fairchild's American Aviation Corporation, and the automobile flavor of the Cord Corporation, all melding somehow down into the General Aviation Corporation, which was converted to the immensely successful North American Aviation under Kindelberger.

The P-51's gene pool is further enriched by its engine, starting with the American Allison, then switching to the Rolls-Royce Merlin, whose own existence can be traced back to the inspiration—or at least the instigation—of the Curtiss V-12! Thus the lovely P-51 Mustangs are the refined product of a rich admixture of almost all of American aviation, and a good bit of German and British as well.

This same vital historic process can be found to greater or lesser degrees in any of the warbirds. The mixed heritage of genius is undoubtedly responsible for the high degree of performance of which the airplanes were capable. This in turn has inspired the legends about them.

Perhaps the best measure of the high level of performance they achieved is found in the unlimited racers, those airplanes that can be improved upon without restriction. Some of the same airframes built in 1944 or 1945 and which began their racing careers in 1946 are still racing today. They are more and more modified, and some of the artisans of refinement talk about the piston-engine Mustang attaining speeds of 600 miles per hour! One can imagine Edgar Schmued looking down with benevolent pride when that happens.

But there are other roads to fame. Boeing B-17s were modified for fire-bombing and served valiantly for years in the toughest of conditions before undergoing restorations. Beech C-45s, after returning to executive service, took on yet another demanding career in flying cargo—chiefly bank checks—at night, in all weather, in all seasons. Transport aircraft drifted into U.S. feeder lines, then migrated to South American lines, often returning many years later on

a one-way trip to an abandoned airstrip carrying the stuff that makes funny cigarettes. And then there are the incredibly resilient T-28 and T-34 trainers that spent years being bounced into the ground by ham-handed student pilots before entering restoration.

Planes have been reclaimed from watery graves, dragged up from years of submersion to be judged worthy of restoration. But there are happier examples too. Some planes were flown for just a few hundred hours and then put into extended storage. When these are discovered, the process of restoration is much easier.

But no matter what the history, no matter what the risk, the real secret of why men and women spend their time and fortunes restoring classic warbirds to flight can only be found in the satisfaction it provides them. To be aware that you have created something of beauty from what was once debris, to know that what you have built is sound and airworthy is a marvelous feeling. To sit at the controls and imagine that you are a famous pilot—Dick Bong, or Don Gentile, or Erich Hartmann—that's worth something, too. But perhaps the best answer can be found in the sparkling eyes of the visitors at Oshkosh, Wisconsin, or at Harlingen, Texas, when they see a warbird for the first time. The tiny, grainy images of airplanes found on T.V. programs like "Twelve O'Clock High" or "Ba Ba Blacksheep" are pale shadows of these big, handsome, capable machines. The veteran planes put flesh to imagination and give depth to history, for they are three-dimensional, filled with sounds, redolent of grease, fuel, and hydraulic fluids. Most vividly of all, they are filled with human spirit.

So in the end, the best analogy to the drive to restore airplanes may be a cocktail. Take one part nostalgia, one part patriotism, two parts craftsmanship, and one part admiration for engineering skills; mix; and garnish with public education and adulation. It's a pretty heady drink, one that will keep the skies filled with classics for years to come.

—WALTER J. BOYNE

was working in a coal mine and attending the Pittsburgh Institute of Aeronautics on weekends. The day after Japan bombed Pearl Harbor, I happened to be at the institute, and my instructor asked me, "Why don't you join the cadets?"

I said, "I don't have any college."

He told me that if I could pass the equivalent of two years of college, I could get in, so right away, I went to the Pittsburgh Post Office and signed up for pilot training as an Army Air Corps cadet. After two months of pre-flight training at Maxwell Field in Montgomery, Alabama, I received the equivalent of two years of college.

When our training was completed, our group went overseas, but my crew was kept behind. They sent us down to Brooksville, Florida, where we were trained to drop glide bombs. You would drop the bombs 20 miles away from the target, and they were supposed to glide on in. We practiced dropping bombs on an uninhabited island in the Bahamas. The month-long glide bombing training was very hush-hush. One guy happened to sneak off the field, and they busted him from second lieutenant down to private just like that.

The B-17 was very easy to fly, and for combat, it was one of the best planes ever built. You could tear that thing half apart, and it would still fly, still respond. We had one guy at our base who was knocked out of formation and German fighters got on him. He out-dove an Fw 190 down to the deck. He had to be doing over 400 mph to out-dive

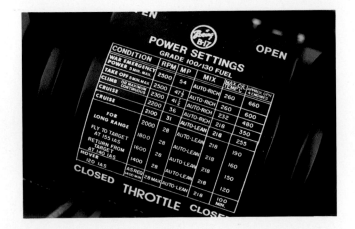

a fighter, but it held together. The B-17 was tough. Even though it looked awkward on the ground, it was a thing of beauty in flight.

Our flying gear included silk gloves with wool gloves over top of them, and leather on top of those two. If the guns jammed up on a high-altitude mission, you might take off the leather and possibly the wool, but you didn't dare take off the silk gloves because your fingers would freeze right to the guns. It was 65 below at times. There was no heat in the plane of any kind, not like these modern planes which are pressurized. And even if it had been pressurized, in combat, one hole would take care of that.

My first raid was out over the North Sea en route to Norway to drop bombs on heavy-water plants there. We didn't encounter any enemy fighters ourselves, although we saw fighters attacking the group ahead of us. Coming back, though, we passed through a heavy rainstorm. There was no way to see through the windshield—we were flying blind. The only way to keep from running into each other was to look out of the windows on the side.

My second mission was close to the west coast of France. There was a boat that had come in from Japan that was supposed to have something on it. We went after that ship but never bombed it because it was too cloudy. Coming back, just before we crossed the English Channel, an enemy fighter came out of the sun. He killed one man and injured three others. One fellow had his boots blown right off him. A shell had exploded—it must have been a 20mm—at the hydraulic pumps alongside him. All of that damage was done on just one pass by the fighter.

After we got back, the tail gunner got out, looked at the tail of the plane, and turned as white as a piece of paper. You would swear that there was no way a human could have been in that tail and not been killed. It had holes all through it. The plane was shot up so bad that they rolled it off the end of the runway and junked it.

If we saw a stray plane coming at us when we were flying formation, everyone put their guns on him. The Germans had captured some of our aircraft, and they would fly up into formation, shoot down a plane, and then take off. If one of our fighters ever pointed his nose at us, we would shoot him. It was self-preservation, because you didn't know if there was a jerry in that plane or a U.S. pilot.

If I'd have kept my mouth shut, I may not have been shot down. We were scheduled to fly a mission to a ball-bearing plant. I was always flying "tail-end Charlie," the most dangerous position in formation. You're the last one, so enemy fighters come in on you first. Before this mission started, I went to the commanding officer and complained. "Damn it," I said, "I'm tired of flying tail-end Charlie." He said that he'd take care of it. I was put on the lead man's right wing.

In formation only two planes carried bomb sights—usually the leader and one of the wingmen. We were on our bomb run, and the lead man called out on the radio, "Bomb sight's out. Take over." It was my 17th mission—February 25, 1944.

No sooner had he said that than I saw one, two, three jerries. They had been tuned in to our radio frequency, and they evidently thought I had the bomb sight, because they were zeroing in on me. They hit my plane with about three shells, which blew it out of formation a half a mile. One shell went up through the right wing. It didn't explode, but the gas drained right out, so we lost an engine. The impact knocked the oil pressure out on the number two inboard engine—I had to feather that one—and we lost the supercharger on the number four engine to a burst underneath it. At that altitude, if you don't have your supercharger, you don't have much power. As a result, we only had one good engine, and we were too far away from our own fighters for protection.

Nine German fighters jumped us. During evasive action, I got down too low and had to land in a big, plowed field. During the landing, I kept hollering over the intercom for the crew to get the ball turret gunner out, which they did. In fact, all ten of us got out all right. No one had a scratch.

Once on the ground, I informed the crew about all the parachutes we had been ducking coming down. A B-24 had been hit, and its crew had bailed out. On our descent, I flew right through them while they were floating through the air, barely missing three of the crewmen.

As we were standing in the field, Germans came in from all directions. They marched us into a town called Landau, where a vehicle picked us up along with what they could find of the B-24 crew. They drove us to one of their prisons. We spent the night there with only a wooden bunk to sleep on and a wooden pillow for a headrest. The next day, they took us to Frankfurt for interrogation, and we stayed there two days. Next, they put us in cattle cars, and shipped us to a town in Germany located right on the Baltic. It was 16 miles from Sweden and freedom, but there was a whole war between us.

At the camp, we weren't physically abused, as far as beatings went, but there was never enough to eat. We found out after the Russians came that the warehouse had been full of Red Cross parcels—spam and chocolate bars and cigarettes—that the Germans had been using for themselves.

Normally, we'd get meat the size of a hamburger for the week. There was a zoo in Berlin, and after the city was bombed, the Germans brought in something we swore was elephant meat, because the bones were so big.

In the morning, they'd boil barley to make cereal. We had two thin slices of bread made out of potato, flour, and sawdust. From time to time, the Germans would bring dehydrated turnips in on a wagon, and we'd be on our hands and knees picking up turnips that had fallen through the cracks in the wagons in order to have something extra to eat. I weighed 195 pounds when I went into the camp, 130 pounds when I came out.

There was some sickness among us, but we had a base doctor in camp. In fact, there was also a catholic priest, so we had medicine, both spiritually and physically.

We wrote letters to the people back home, but they were unsealed and about the size of an envelope, so you couldn't say much. At least our families knew we were alive.

The Germans had a shoemaker shop in prison camp, and they asked for people who could resole shoes to work in it. I'd done a little bit—living through the Depression, you had to—so I volunteered. The Red Cross furnished the leather, and we punched an awl through the leather to make a hole for the wooden nails they sent us. It was better than walking barefoot!

One time I concocted a scheme for prisoners to escape. At a prearranged signal, guys would throw mush balls—we had some athletic equipment—into the area between each guard tower and the high fence where they had barbed wire. This would draw the attention of the guards. Then the guy would say he wanted to get the ball inside the barbed wire fence. These guys would hop over the barbed wire, and naturally, the guards would be watching them getting the ball out while another group of guys would go scurrying over and escape. I think we got three or four out the first night, and three or four out the second night.

One morning after I was there 14 or 15 months, we discovered that the Germans had taken off during the night. They had heard that the Russians were in the area,

and they were scared to death of them.

Once the Russians took over the camp, you could leave if you wanted to, but they brought in cows and pigs that they'd taken from local farmers, so many people stayed because of the food. Some guys went into the towns. In fact, the natives invited our boys to stay with them, because if an American boy was in their house, the Russians wouldn't bother them.

We stayed with the Russians three or four weeks. One day, B-17s, one after the other, came in and hauled us out to France. I think they moved the whole camp out in about a day—27,000 people. They put us on a train and took us to Camp Lucky Strike. There, the guys went down and traded packs of cigarettes for white bread. That white bread was like cake to us.

All they fed us at Camp Lucky Strike was creamed food. Our stomachs were not fit to eat anything else like potatoes and steaks—just creamed beef and creamed chicken. We tore the camp apart the three or four weeks we spent there waiting to go home.

Finally, "General Ike," General Eisenhower, came. He landed, stood up on the wing of his airplane, and said, "We're doing everything in our power to get you home as fast as we can, so be patient." And about a week later a brand-new boat came over. We loaded all the guys on it. We were sleeping on the deck and every place else. Halfway back, the steering malfunctioned, and we circled around and around and around in the middle of the ocean for half a day or better. The boat finally arrived in Boston, and from there I went home.

Joseph S. Bochna flew a B-17 Flying Fortress with the 526th Squadron, 379th Bombardment Group (Heavy), 8th Army Air Force. Shot down over Germany on his 17th combat mission, he spent 14 months in a prisoner-of-war camp. He received the Air Medal with two Oak Leaf Clusters.

riefly we were assigned a B-24 that we called the "Silver Ghost." It was one of the first non-camouflaged planes in our squadron. There was a great deal of anxiety about flying that silver plane because we thought it would expose us in the air. There we were flying in formation with all these drab-painted B-24s and our ship was glinting in the sunlight, spotting us for the enemy fighters. We felt we had been discriminated against when they assigned it to us. Fortunately, nothing happened. Shortly afterwards, we were assigned "Tailwind," the camouflaged ship in which I flew most of my missions.

Our intelligence officers briefed us on what to expect before each mission—approximately when we would encounter fighters, how many we might expect, the amount of ground fire we would experience. I must say that our intelligence wasn't always as good as we felt it should be. Often they'd say, "Well, you'll encounter light flak," or, "You'll have few, if any, fighters," and you'd go out and the fighters would be in abundance and you'd never seen so much flak in your life!

The enemy would try to break us up before we got to our target. If we hit the target, the fighters really came in, because we'd done some damage. We could have the tightest formation, and they would still come dead on to us, blasting away. They shot windshields out, and there would be flak all over the place. The most intense flak was located around any type of manufacturing—steelworks, oil fields—and around airdromes and marshaling yards.

We flew in clements of six: a lead ship, a right and a left wingman, and then three planes below that would fit up under the lead group. We stayed in close formation to be as exact as we could in pattern bombing. We weren't trying to hit single buildings. We bombed the airdromes as soon as we hit the beginning of the airfields. We'd fly with another group next to us which allowed us to cover the whole thing.

With a tight formation, we also had more concentrated firepower. Instead of confronting the enemy with a top turret, a couple of waist guns, a tail gun, or the nose gun of a single bomber, we shot from all the planes. Enemy fighters who flew into that fire were taking real chances, but there were some daredevils.

Fighters coming at us would split. They'd come in from the sun, so that it was difficult to see them, or they would come from around clouds, frequently coming over the clouds instead of under them. I even had fighters fly straight through our formation, guns firing. One made a pass so close to my cockpit that I'm sure that if I had seen the pilot walking around down on the ground later, I would've recognized him.

It was difficult to fly into the concentrations of flak. But when you were flying into a pattern, you couldn't break formation, because you might fly into someone else, or you wouldn't drop your bomb load effectively, so you wouldn't be doing your job. And anti-aircraft guns were shooting from many areas on the ground, so you might leave one area only to fly into another that was worse. You knew you were going to lose a certain number of airplanes and men one way or another, but you never had the feeling that it could happen to you. Maybe before a mission, or during the night when you had time to think, you might wonder. But from the time you went to your briefing until the time you got back from your mission, you were so busy that you had to concentrate on what you were doing, and you didn't have time to feel any fear.

The most concentrated, low-level bombing occurred at the abbey of Cassino, Italy. We had been flying two missions a day in a maximum effort to break through the lines there. Our ground troops had reached a stalemate with the Germans and could not get into the town. A decision was made to destroy the town completely, including the abbey, because the Germans were using it as a base of operations.

We flew in low, about 1,500 feet—a "buzz job" as we called it—and encountered no enemy opposition, only slight, inaccurate flak.

Later that week I drove through Cassino, or what was left of it. The ruins were still smoking, and there weren't two blocks left standing together. It was utter devastation.

The worst raids were over the Bucharest and Ploesti areas, as well as a couple of missions in Munich. When we traveled to Bad Voslau, one of Hitler's main encampments, it was a long mission for us. There was heavy opposition all the way. The closer we got into those central areas, the worse the flak and fighters became.

The missions into Ploesti and Bucharest were easily eight- or nine-hour missions, our maximum range. Normally, we didn't fly the shortest distance by going directly from one point to another, but when we flew into Ploesti and Bucharest, we went as directly as we could because of limited fuel supply. If we couldn't get to our target due to bad weather, we hit alternate targets. We also flew to mislead the enemy so they didn't know which target we were actually going to hit. Intelligence would say we were going one place, and the next thing we knew, we were making a 45- or 90-degree change.

If a couple of engines were shot out or other damage occurred during our longer missions, we didn't stand a chance of making it back to base, because we encountered a lot of fighters. If our engines were shot, we got rid of everything except some ammunition. Sometimes it only took a few shots to frighten away the enemy fighters. Closer in, say, with only an hour's flying time left, we could get crippled up and still get back.

Every time we saw one of our planes out of control or smoking, we'd watch very carefully and count to see if ten chutes came out, assuming that there were ten men in each one. When we got back, we'd be debriefed. By putting all the information from the debriefing sessions together, the intelligence officers could estimate pretty accurately the results of the mission.

The B-24 was a "hot" plane. We went 120 to 125 miles per hour taking off, and when we came in, we landed under power. We hit the ground at around 110 miles per hour. I never had a runway that was too long!

It took longer to get off the dirt runways in Italy, because a lot of gravel bits got in our props when we were taking off and landing. We couldn't abort takeoff, except at a very early point. So if we got up and were really rolling, there was no way to stop. Fortunately, these planes had marvelous engines, and we seldom had a failure.

It's remarkable that with all those takeoffs and landings, many of them occurring when my ship was full of holes or flying with reduced power—I think that we had more three-engine time than any other airplane in the squadron due either to mechanical failure or battle damage—the landing the members of my crew and I remember most vividly is our return from Cairo, Egypt. We had flown there on leave after Rome had been taken, and of course, you can get some of the best Scotch whiskey in the world in Cairo. When the other men in the squadron found out where we were going, a number of them chipped in money and placed their orders. Coming back from Cairo, I figured that I had better "grease one on," because we had about $2,000 worth of Scotch whiskey in the bomb bay and I knew if I broke even one bottle I would be in big trouble. My crewmen still joke about that being the smoothest landing I ever made.

Axis Sally would broadcast for the enemy on the radio all the time overseas. Frequently, she would tell her listeners where we were going the next day and what our exact target was going to be—and she was accurate! She would report on how many bombers we had lost, that the enemy had interrogated some of the flight crews on the ground, and that our men had claimed they were glad to be in the hands of the Germans! We listened to her regularly just out of curiosity. It was sometimes startling that she could be as accurate as she was on so many things. On some of the earlier missions, we were concerned about how the enemy was getting information, but it could have been simple guesswork. They knew, for example, that if we missed an important target one day, we had to go back to it the next.

There were four squadrons to every group, and we knew most of them fairly well, because we flew wing-to-wing with them. We trained as a crew and got to be almost like a family. Great respect existed between the enlisted men and the officers. It took my men a long time to get to the point where they could call me by my first name, even though I was pretty easy to get along with. We ran a tight ship, with a lot of discipline on the plane.

When I came back from overseas, I got a green instrument-flight card, which was comparable to an airline-pilot's license in those days. I worked at a factory in Michigan that was making B-24s. The United States was shipping 24s all over the world before the end of the war. The engineering department at the plant would develop specifications on how various parts of the plane were supposed to perform, and I had the responsibility of verifying those figures.

A plane was pulled off the line at random, and I would take it out to a designated field, test it, and then it would be ferried to its final destination. When I was testing the engineers' specs, I would fly the plane precisely the way they told me to. It was interesting work and enabled me to fly all over the country.

F. Bradley Peyton III was the pilot of a B-24 Liberator with the 738th Squadron, 454th Bombardment Group (Heavy), 15th Army Air Force. He flew 38 combat missions, 13 of which were double-credit missions. He was awarded the Distinguished Flying Cross with Cluster, the Air Medal with seven Oak Leaf Clusters, and the President's Distinguished Unit Citation (twice).

Evolved from commercial aircraft, the C-47 was built for military purposes, with big doors, strong walls, and tie-down placements for cargo. My C-47 was equipped with four 100-gallon gasoline tanks bolted down on each side of the cabin. It was a reliable and durable airplane. We used to say you could fly it into the ground, and it would bounce back like a ball.

We'd fly from India to China across the Himalayas—the "Hump"—at an altitude of 17,000 feet. Each base along the way had a radio beacon. You'd home in on the signal, land, and unload your cargo.

Weather was always a problem. Back then, no one knew about jet streams. Pilots would often find themselves over their target 40 minutes ahead of schedule, or their instruments would show that enough time had elapsed to reach their destination, when actually the base was still ahead. Confused, pilots flew off course, trying to verify their position. They would come down from the clouds to look and end up flying into mountainsides or deviating off course so much that they ran out of fuel. We lost many airplanes and crews.

One day they brought in a new airplane, the C-46, which was supposed to carry twice the weight of a C-47. It had higher lift-capacity and a bigger engine and body. We used it to haul gasoline and ammunition.

While good for heavy airlifts, the C-46 had some problems. Its loading doors were placed too high for easy access, the throttle drifted out of position, and oil congealed in the engines at high altitudes. Transport ability was needed so badly at that time that the engineers bypassed normal testing procedures.

I was flying a C-46 over the Hump with 23 barrels of fuel strapped inside the day I went down. The fuel pressure began to fluctuate in my left engine; then the engine caught on fire, so I shut it down.

Flying with only one engine and carrying heavy cargo, the airplane wouldn't climb. In fact, the remaining engine was heating up from the strain, so I started losing altitude. Heavy cloud-cover prevented me from knowing how close I was to the ridge, but I knew I couldn't stay at 11,000 feet and clear it, so I ordered the crew to bail out.

Everyone jumped out but the radio operator. He couldn't get his parachute on—the straps wouldn't loosen. Now, I was faced with a choice. I could bail out and leave the rascal to die, stay in the airplane and die with him, or maybe, somehow, luck out.

The ridges off the Himalayas run straight north and south, with wide valleys between them. If we were over one of those valleys, there was a chance I could fly the airplane south until the ridges got smaller, cross at 4,000 feet, and head back into India.

The clouds finally broke, and I could see that we were between two ridges. To decrease the airplane's weight, the radio operator cut loose the barrels of gasoline and rolled them out the door. Even with an empty plane, however, the engine was as hot as a pistol. I was losing altitude, and we were only a few hundred feet from the ground.

The radio operator finally got his chute on, and I told him to bail out. I set the airplane on a course to fly into the ridge, raced down the cabin, and dived out behind him. As my parachute was snapping open, I realized that the ground was very close. I could see the tops of trees and an open field, with burned-off stumps on it. I hit the ground right in the middle of that clearing. The blow just about knocked me silly.

I unbuckled my chute, looked up at the top of the hill, and noticed a native. I had no way of knowing whether he was friend or foe. He didn't say anything. He just stood there. I crawled up the bank towards him and asked if he spoke English. He shook his head no.

Down on the far end of the clearing, I spotted my radio operator and another man walking out of the jungle. My crewman was all scratched up because he'd hit a tree on the way down.

The natives took us to a bamboo shack. I removed an aeronautical chart from my jacket and spread it out, indicating that I wanted to go north to a base with a landing strip and a radio station. Of course, I didn't know exactly where it was, or how long it would take to get there.

We stayed in the shack overnight and left the next morning with the natives as our guides. They led us up a very steep ridge, on a trail with short zig-zags. At the top, we found a little village, and that was where we spent the night. By then I was exhausted, because I wasn't used to mountain-climbing.

In that shack, I took stock of another problem. My radio operator was wearing low-quarter shoes and the soles were worn completely through. We had a lot of walking to do, and soon his feet would be lacerated all over. We decided to make new insoles from some of the parachute webbing.

On the fourth day, we met a group of men on the trail. The leader could speak a few words of English. He knew where I wanted to go and indicated it would take about 15 days. Then he wrote down the names of villages, each a day's walk from the other. He also gave me 20 to 25 small chunks of a substance that looked like tar but smelled just like a freshly dug tree-root. I found out later it was crude opium. We used it on our trip as payment to the leader of each village who gave us shelter for the night.

One day our lookout spotted a Japanese patrol at the top of a hill. We hid, but I knew that if the patrol discovered American shoe-tracks, we would be caught. It was a very tense situation. After an hour and a half, the guide took another look. He returned and told us that the patrol had gone, so we proceeded up the ridge. At the top we discovered a second trail, which branched off in a different direction and which the Japanese patrol had taken. It was pure, blind luck that saved our hides that day.

After 16 or 17 days, we arrived at a village, and the leader handed me an envelope. Inside was a note from a British troop commander, and he informed me that we were only two or three days south of his location. The natives had sent a courier ahead, and that's how he knew we were coming.

The Special Forces had coordinated a rescue plan with native leaders, where we supplied the natives with weapons and ammunition, and they rescued crews that bailed out. Since the invasion of Burma was being planned, their help was essential. Undoubtedly, the arrangement saved our lives.

After 20 days we reached our destination, and I learned that the rest of my crew had made it back safely, too. At that time, we were only the second crew to have gone down in the Himalayas and come out of the jungle alive.

Matt Carmack was a check pilot who flew both the C-47 and C-46 over the "Hump." His assignments included the 1st Ferrying Group, 13th Ferrying Squadron; the 22nd Ferrying Group, 78th Ferrying Squadron; the India-China Wing, 1st and 13th Transport Squadrons; the India-China Wing, 1st Transport Group, 6th Transport Squadron; the India-China Wing, 303rd Transport Squadron; and the India-China Wing, Air Transport Command. He was awarded the Distinguished Flying Cross, the Air Medal, and the President's Distinguished Unit Citation.

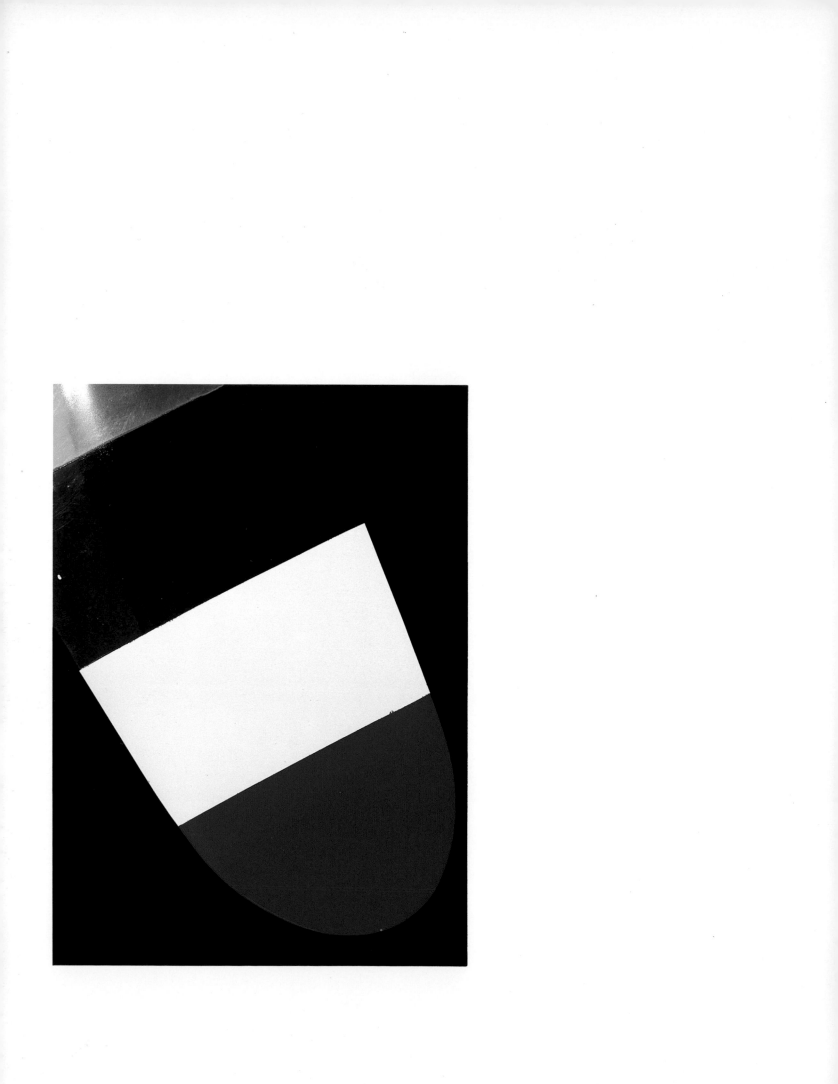

When I graduated from law school in July 1941, I knew I was going into the armed services somewhere, because of selective service. I had come up with a very low draft number, and I decided I'd better make my own choice.

I ended up in the 71st Fighter Squadron, North African Strategic Air Force. There were 13 of us sent over to West Africa on New Year's Eve, 1943, to replace pilots that were lost during the invasion of Africa. I was stationed in Ain-M'Lila, Algeria, which is at the northern head of the Sahara Desert, and I flew 50 missions from there before I came back home in July.

The first mission I remember very well. It was called Biskra, and we were strafing Rommel's troops as they were coming out of Libya. That was in January 1943. We flew north toward Libya along the Mediterranean.

We flew in formation and machine-gunned trucks and tanks and the soldiers that were traveling along with them. Then we got attacked by Me 109s. We lost one fellow, not because he got hit by a fighter, but because he got so low, he flew into a telephone pole.

The Me 109 was a very effective fighter. We ran into a lot of them. I remember one briefing where three of our squadrons were preparing for a mission to bomb a couple of airfields. The intelligence officer who was briefing us said, "In this one field over here there are 142 Me 109s, and in the other field there are 60 more Me 109s," and some jokester in the back of the room said, "And there are 202 of them coming in at 12 o'clock." No matter where we went, it seemed we were outnumbered three-quarters of the time.

When Rommel tried to break through the Kasserine Pass, the Allies had every airplane in North Africa flying through and shooting at whatever was on the ground. Rommel's gunners were up in the hills, shooting down at us, which was a disconcerting experience. That's why I don't fly anymore. I figure I've used up all the luck I ever had.

When Rommel tried to get out of North Africa, the Germans sent everything that could transport anything over to fly out Rommel's troops. We intercepted probably 300 airplanes in the Mediterranean. Everything was there. You'd fly along and see Germans flying past you. Everybody was going everywhere in every direction. I don't think anybody knew what was going on, but we slaughtered them.

I was the lead man on that mission. We were flying on the deck, having been assigned slightly different altitudes. When we found a German aircraft, we shot him. Meanwhile, you kept looking back to make sure they didn't get on your tail. There were so many airplanes there—it was incredible. I imagine we shot down close to 100 aircraft that day.

We didn't make passes, just engaged and kept going. There were too many airplanes around to make passes. I'd see somebody coming in and turn my nose right at him, as did the whole squadron. You'd fire as the enemy was going by, but you didn't see him again, because he'd either be headed somewhere else, or he'd be going down dead. Generally, they don't turn back once they know you've seen them. The best defense a fighter pilot has is to see the other plane before it sees him, or at least before it can get within firing range.

The P-38 was beautiful. Ours carried four 50-caliber

machine guns and one 20mm cannon. Depending on the mission, we'd sometimes carry two 500-pound bombs, or one bomb and one belly tank. If we were going on high-altitude assignments escorting B-17s, we might carry two belly tanks.

The P-38 was unique because it had a steering wheel rather than a stick. Of course, you had control of your ailerons, and when you pushed the column back and forth, it put you up and down.

Firing controls for the machine guns were separate from the cannon. The button for the machine guns was on the top of the steering column, while the cannon controls were on the bottom. You could fire the bullets as tracers out of the machine guns and when you saw they were going in the right direction, you'd use your cannon. I don't think I shot the cannon much at all. I employed it more for ground-support activity since it had greater firepower and would do more damage.

In combat the Lightning had a great advantage in torque. The aircraft had counter-rotating propellers, which meant we could turn very tightly in either direction. Other airplanes could be turned tightly with their torque, but if they were turned against it, they had trouble.

I remember when we left advanced training to go and check out the Lightning, all the boys were telling us that it was dangerous to fly—that you couldn't parachute out.

Inverting the aircraft was one theory for bailing out, but another way was to slow the P-38 down just as slow as you could get it, then get out on the wing, slide on the wing to get down below the boom, and drop. I never wanted to test it, but I knew some fellows who had gotten out that way, so I knew it could be done. The trouble with inverting an airplane and dropping out of it was that there was a good chance that the airplane might continue on its arc, which meant it could end up circling under you as you were para-chuting down.

One of the closest calls I had was when we were escort-ing B-17s in Tunis. There were enemy fighters all over the B-17s, and we were trying to keep them off. The enemy shot down at least one plane and started going after the crewmen who had bailed out. As I pulled out to chase the fighters away from the fellows in parachutes, I looked behind me, and there were two Me 109s back on my left tail, and two more on my right. I was at about 18,000 feet. To avoid them I just went straight down, diving, sweeping the plane back and forth to avoid their fire. I pulled out at about 2,500 feet. When I looked around, there was no one near me.

Unfortunately, by that time I had lost one engine and the whole electrical system of the plane. I had one hole in the canopy, where a bullet had come in behind me and had hit the instrument panel. I flew for a little bit, and then I saw a B-17 heading west. I managed to get my plane up very cautiously underneath the B-17—the gunner saw me coming, but I didn't go rushing in—and I flew underneath that 17 until we were almost to the home base, so that I'd have someone else shooting if there was need for it.

Then I flew over the base, making the normal pattern to land. That's when I found out that my two main wheels wouldn't go down. Only the nose wheel did. I know all the people on the P-38 side of the field saw the trouble I was in, but the bombers used the same field. When I was coming in for final approach, I saw a bomber coming in the other way on the same runway. So I flew my plane down hard into the ground, and that broke the nose wheel, then I bounced back up. I came down, hit the ground, and slid right under the B-17's wing. I didn't fly for two weeks after that incident. It was a hell of a way to land a P-38, but it gave me a lot of confidence in the airplane. I never worried about the Lightning after that.

We got a potful of flying in the invasion of Sicily. We flew two missions a day—once it was three missions in a day. We'd take off at some ungodly hour, go over and do our job, come home, refuel, take off, go back over. During all this time, we'd get out of the plane for 45 minutes, maybe an hour. Missions were constant. Every two or three days, we were totally engaged.

It was a hard life. I was the right age at the time to put up with it. We were on British rations, which meant we got tea with milk in it, mutton about every other meal, and a quart of scotch and gin each month, which only lasted a couple days. Socializing meant either poker or volleyball.

As for gear, sometimes I wore an oxygen mask when flying over 10,000 feet, but we had no anti-g suits. There was weather flying gear, and it was occasionally required, but I preferred not to wear it because it was so bulky. I usually wore just a khaki shirt and trousers, a parachute, a gun, and a canteen. That was it.

I don't ever remember seeing people on the ground. Our primary target on strafing runs was almost always planes on airfields, with the exception of the Kasserine Pass, which was a "must" operation—Rommel was about to break loose and screw up all our plans for trapping him. There I remember strafing troops. Outside of that, our targets were either trucks, airplanes, or tanks. Undoubtedly, people were in them, but you could never allow yourself to think about that. That's one reason I never wanted to be in the infantry. It's possible I killed a number of people. My God, but you had to do it.

I don't think anyone liked strafing. You did it, but you didn't necessarily have to love it. It was one of the worst things you could do, because you knew someone was going to be shooting at you while you were at it.

I remember one time when we were strafing—we were coming back from a bombing mission in Sicily, and there were anti-aircraft guns down below shooting at us. I looked back and saw their tracers going in between the booms of my airplane. I got 72 holes in my Lightning that day.

Once I was a Canadian prisoner. I had gotten separated on a mission coming off a target, and I was flying into the coast of Africa by myself with very little gasoline, when I saw an airstrip. I landed very nicely, happy to have the thing on the ground. Then I raised my canopy, took off my parachute, climbed out on the wing, and a man said, "Put your hands up." Here was this Canadian sergeant with a .45 aimed at me.

I tried to explain to him who I was, but there were other instances of Germans coming into fields. It would take time to confirm my identity, so I spent the night in jail. That evening I had a couple of beers with the Canadians, and we talked. They asked me a lot of questions about the United States, and I'm sure that before the night was over, they were convinced I was a Yank. The next morning they gassed up my plane, and I flew on down to my airfield. That was the only time I was "captured" during the war.

Henry R. Beeson was a P-38 Lightning pilot with the 71st Squadron, 1st Fighter Group, North African Strategic Air Force. He flew 50 combat missions and was awarded the distinguished Flying Cross and the Air Medal with six Oak Leaf Clusters.

Before I went into the service—before the war started, for that matter—I had a girl that I was going with pretty regularly. We were driving to a dance at the country club. It was just the two of us in the car, and I was feeling good, so I asked, "Do you know what I'd like to be doing right now?"

She batted her eyelashes and leaned real close to me and said, "No, what would you like to be doing?"

"I'd like to be at the controls of a powerful fighter plane."

"Oh," she said, and then moved over to the other side of the car. I had always wanted to fly, you see. Although I named my airplane overseas after the girl, that night was pretty much the end of our relationship.

In the open-cockpit airplanes when I first reported to flying school in 1943, the instructor had a gosport in the front cockpit. It was a tube that looked like a stethoscope. The instructor kept the long end and you fastened the ear pieces inside your helmet. That way the instructor could talk to you, but you couldn't talk back. He watched you in his mirror up front, and if you didn't do what he told you to do, or if you didn't know how to do what he told you, he'd yell in your ear.

The instructors were always chewing at you. For instance, this one student only came down to an altitude of 820 feet after his instructor had told him to hold at 800. So the instructor hit the stick and yelled, "Get down there!" The student didn't have his safety belt fastened, so he fell out of his seat and slid backwards with the slipstream, until he was straddling the rudder. The Stearman, the airplane we were trained in, had a skin made of tough fabric, but this guy was so scared that he punched his fingers right through the material and wrapped them around the launcher rods. In the meantime, the instructor took the plane up to 2,000 feet, pulled back on the throttle, and started calling to the student, "Come on up! Come on up!" But the kid wouldn't move, so the instructor had to land with him hanging on

that way. The story made the local newspapers!

After training at Thunderbird in Phoenix, Arizona, I was sent over to Luke Field for advanced training. One day a couple of the biggest, darkest airplanes I had ever seen came in and landed. They were P-47s painted olive drab. P-47s were fairly new then, so we ran down to base operations to see them.

A little guy got out of the cockpit and climbed down one, two, three, four steps to the ground. We stood there waiting for the rest of the people to get out of that big airplane, but there wasn't anybody else. I thought, "Boy, this little guy gets to fly that big fighter all by himself!"

Not long after receiving my commission as second lieutenant, I was sent to England. It was 1944. The base, Martlesham Heath Aerodrome, near Ipswich, was old. It had once been a grass field like most other British airfields, but when we brought over the B-17 and B-24 bombers, they decided to pave the landing strip. In order to make the 6,000-foot runway that was needed, they had to cross over a major highway. They put gates on the road with a guard, and when an airplane was going to take off, the gates would come down like they do at a railroad crossing.

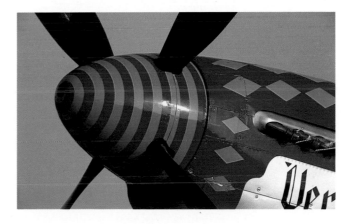

We lived in a British barracks that had three wings and looked like an "E" from the air. Normally, only one man was assigned to a room, but we were assigned doubles. When you put two beds in a room, you had just enough room for a wardrobe. The room had a fireplace because there was no central heating. Each barracks wing had a bat-man. Ours had served with Lord Kitchener. He was named "Robbie," short for Robinson, and was probably 70 years old. He had a little white moustache, an oval-shaped face, and would say "Very good, sir," just like the butlers you see in the movies.

When I first came to the squadron, a veteran pilot came into my quarters. He tried to light a cigarette, but his hands were shaking so badly that he could hardly get it lit. He told me how bad it was out there, but I figured that I was getting the "new kid" treatment, so I was curt with the guy. As it turned out, he wasn't joking. Seven men had reported to the squadron after D-Day, and only three were left. He was one of them. On his airplane he had written "The Lord is my Shepherd." He was a strange case. We used to tease him by arguing about which one of us would get his new boots after he was shot down. Black humor was our way of dealing with death.

The winter of 1944-45 was the worst in England in 50 years. It was cold, and there were low ceilings. We wore gabardine wool uniforms that we lined with parachute silk to keep the uniform from scratching and cutting our skin. The boots issued to us were brown, but we polished them black so that they wouldn't give us away to the Germans, who wore black brogans. We also wore a pair of wool socks over a pair of cotton ones so that our feet wouldn't freeze when we were flying. The heaters in the aircraft were very bad, and ice would often form inside the cockpit.

One event I remember very clearly was when our squadron was converted from the P-47 Thunderbolt to the P-51 Mustang. Our airfield was located right inside the German buzz-bomb area, so the British shot down anything in a 4,000-foot-altitude by two-square-mile area. Therefore, when we flew in, we came in very high. One day, from way up there, we saw P-51s sitting by the runway. Our com-

manding officer was the only guy who knew we were switching over.

It was a radical change. We had been used to flying the P-47, which was a plane that we knew would bring us back. The P-47 was tough. On one mission, I was over "mat-tress"—heavy overcast—at about 10,000 feet when I saw bursts of flak around us and realized that we had flown straight for too long. Normally, we would do S-turns to avoid flak, because if you ever heard it, it was almost certain to get you. I heard a click and smoke poured into the cockpit. It cleared, so everything was okay, but when we got back to land, I discovered that my hydraulic system had been shot out.

We were a little unsure about the new P-51s. To ease our fears, they brought in George Preddy, the leading P-51 ace in the European Theater, to show us what the airplane could do. We all lined up by the airfield and watched Preddy take off. He did a roll right after takeoff with the landing gear still down, and we all thought, "Wow! That's an air-plane." The P-51 had tremendous power.

Our basic job was to escort B-24 Liberators and B-17 Flying Fortresses. On my second mission in the P-51, we were following our bombers east and had just gotten our feet dry—that meant we were over occupied enemy territory. (We "got our feet wet" as we flew over the English Channel.) We had mounted 16 airplanes, when "Nuthouse," the radar guy in our group, first reported 15-20 jerry fighters, then 20-30 more. Then he said there might be 60-70 jerries.

We were flying at 25,000 feet at full throttle when my lead reported that he couldn't drop his external tanks. The tanks were made of resinated paper so that the Germans wouldn't have salvage material when we dropped them. He couldn't get the switch, which was down in the front of the cockpit, to move. The external tank ran dry, and his engine stopped at about 400 miles per hour. His wing man lost him as he dropped into the haze, so I followed him down,

down, until he got his engine started again at about 700 feet over German countryside. His switch had frozen at altitude, the ice turning to slush as he dropped.

The cold temperatures at high altitudes were a problem with the new P-51s. Many of the guys were fighting with no guns or partial guns, because the grease used in them was too heavy for the cold. We could hear the fight going on all around us all the time as my lead man lost altitude. The actual number, as it turned out, was 150 German aircraft.

As strange as it probably sounds, combat was the best job I ever had. I looked forward to it. Our flight commander made up the roster, which could change during the night. A flight surgeon or intelligence officer would roust us out of bed about 5 a.m. That's when we would find out whether we were flying a mission that day. If we were, we'd get dressed and go over to group operations where we were briefed on the points of attack, destination, weather conditions, expected enemy resistance, and so on.

In the English winter, it would still be dark when we went to breakfast. We'd be issued eggs, which we carried over to the cook to prepare. By that time the bombers were already airborne. The air would be filled with their roaring, and they would shoot off red buncher flares to form boxes—formations of 12. It's hard to describe the incredible sound they made in the air. There might be 1,000 bombers up at one time, in a line maybe ten miles long.

After breakfast, we'd play bridge or ping-pong. Then we'd go to lockers and suit up. "Doc" Higgins, the flight surgeon, always drove us out to the airplanes. Then a signal flare would fire from the tower, and they would get us going right away.

We flew toward a rendezvous point where we would meet up with the bombers in about an hour or two. On what we called "persistent contrail days," the engines on the bombers formed cylindrical clouds 10-12 miles long at 20,000 feet, so it was easy for us to track them. Unfortunately, it made it easy for the enemy fighters as well. Once we had made the rendezvous, we'd start essing over the box formation, with some fighters going out ahead to intercept, while others provided close cover.

As the bombers approached their target, we broke off, waiting outside the bombing area. It is hard to believe the flak patterns they flew into. I remember seeing one B-24 explode in the air. It was simply there one minute and gone the next. I was one mile away and saw its wings floating down, its four engines smoking and falling rapidly. I saw three parachutes appear, but the chutes were smoking. They started falling faster and faster. I couldn't take my eyes off them.

A. Hess Bomberger flew 66 missions in P-47 Thunderbolts and P-51 Mustangs with the 361st Fighter Squadron, 356th Fighter Group, 8th Army Air Force. He received the Distinguished Flying Cross, the Air Medal with six Oak Leaf Clusters, along with other military decorations.

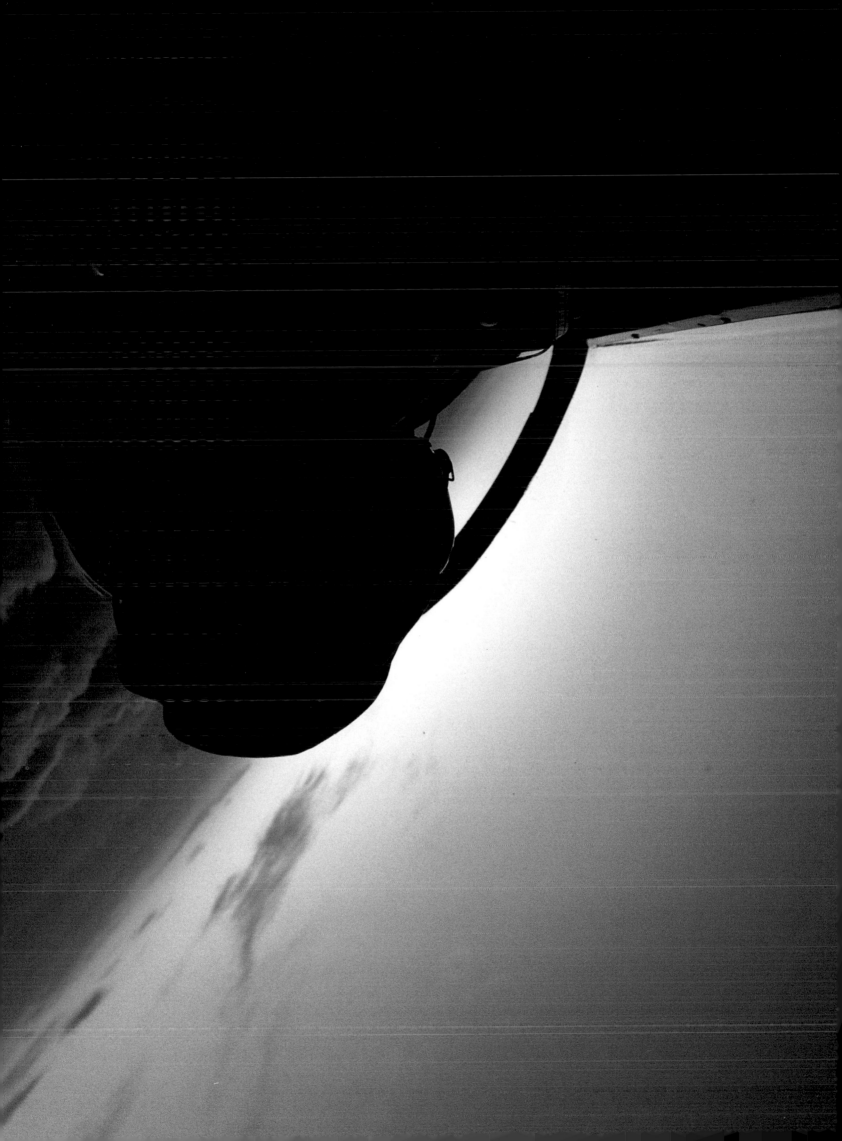

Looking back on it, Navy training was outstanding. When you graduated from Pensacola, you were qualified in everything—torpedo bombing, dive bombing, gunnery, and horizontal bombing—before you went to the fleet. Going out there and shooting gunnery every day and competing with each other—it was just a great life. Afterwards I was assigned to the *Saratoga,* flying torpedo bombers.

In 1941 I was recruited for the American Volunteer Group (AVG), better known as the "Flying Tigers." I had come down off a flight with a couple of my buddies in Norfolk, and we had just walked in the door when the gunnery squadron officer said, "Here's a couple of guys who will go with you." We didn't know what he was talking about. Then we saw a commander. He pulled down a map and said, "This is Burma. This is the Burma Road. We need some people to keep that road open." The three of us didn't even know where Burma was, but we were inseparable friends. We said that we would go.

Right after that the *Saratoga* moved out to Bermuda to help the British. Their convoys would make up in Bermuda, and our planes would go out ahead of them and run search curves for submarines. On one of our trips, we located two submarines and a tender. The submarines were up on the surface refueling when we caught them. The British task force on the aircraft carrier *Eagle* came steaming over. When they finished, there was nothing but oil and debris floating in a circle in the ocean.

Once we took off for Bermuda, we didn't think any more about our conversation with the commander. We were sure the Navy would never release us because they were trying to expand the fleet. If we left, the experience level would be cut pretty thin. Our skipper flew up to Washington to block our release because we were the only carrier that was trained and ready to go to war, but when the skipper came back, he said, "I don't know what's going on, but you're leaving."

To join the AVG we had to have civilian status. So we resigned our Navy commissions, and lost a year of service in the process. Our skipper gave us a big party, and we were off. We shipped out of San Francisco on a Dutch ship with an Indonesian crew carrying half missionaries and half AVG guys. Boy, was it wild. I don't know who converted whom on that ship.

We traveled from San Francisco to Australia and then on up to Malaysia and then to Rangoon. Conditions at the base where we trained were primitive. It had been a British base, but they abandoned it in the summertime because it was so bad—insects like you can't believe, bugs of all kinds everywhere. You'd have to cover your food with an extra plate, or else the maggots would fill the plate up. The only escape from the insects was at night when you got under the mosquito netting around your bunk. There were very few supplies, particularly after Burma fell, so we were short on everything.

The Flying Tiger operation was structured like this. There was a company called Central Aircraft Manufacturing Company owned by William D. Pauley, and we were under contract to him. Bill Pauley was an old China-hand and had the Curtiss franchise out there to sell planes. We loaned money to the Chinese so that they could finance the operation. They did all the recruiting, paid our salaries, and bought our airplanes—100 B-model P-40s.

There was no rank; we only had pay grades. In addition to our salaries, we got a $500 bonus for each airplane that we shot down. It was a gentleman's agreement—nothing was written in our contract—but they honored it and paid off on 286 airplanes.

Discipline in the squadron was fairly lax, but we knew we had a job to do. Since we knew that our lives depended on teamwork, there was high *esprit de corps.*

The secret to our success was our training and the way

we used the P-40. Even though it was a doggy kind of airplane, it was very good for the environment if it was used properly. The P-40 had speed in a dive, and its wings were stressed for heavy g's. Japanese pilots who tried to follow us often would rip the wings right off their airplanes. We'd just roll the plane over in a dive, do about a half roll going straight down, and then pull out on a different heading. The Japanese would be lost behind us. The P-40's weakness was that it couldn't turn inside of a Japanese airplane, so he'd get right on your tail. You couldn't dogfight with the Japanese in a P-40.

Another secret to our success was our high mobility. We could move a squadron from central Burma all the way to east China in a matter of a day. The Japanese could never quite figure out how many airplanes we had. We were so highly mobile that we could move into and out of the action quickly.

Our main tactic was the two-ship element. In the Navy, everybody was flying what is called an ABC formation—a three-ship formation, which was very unwieldy. But the two-ship formation was different. If you had six planes, the first two would go in, hit the Japanese fighters, and pull them off. Then the second two would go in and hit the Japanese bombers. The third two would stay up, case the situation, and provide cover.

Japanese pilots were good. If they weren't disturbed, their raids would come off perfectly. The problem with them was that they couldn't accommodate unusual situations, so once you broke them up, they'd be lost. Their bombers would stay in a big V formation and would never break it. We'd start right in on the back of them, and they'd still hold together, down to the last one. Sometimes the Japanese had as many as 100 fighters and bombers going up. When you engaged in that situation, it was unbelievable. It was like a beehive, with airplanes buzzing everywhere.

One morning we got word that the Japanese had bombed Kunming, the capital of the Hunan province. Our squadron deployed immediately and arrived in Kunming by five o'clock that afternoon. It was our first trip to China. We landed in a grass field near the town.

Kunming was the first time I really saw what war is all about. The Japanese bombers had come in and bombed the town, even though there was no military target there. They had no fighter escorts; they had just bombed for practice. There were two or three hundred bodies lying around, and all these people were outside trying to identify their kin and clean up the mess. It really got my attention.

The next morning the Japanese bombers came back, but we intercepted them about 40 miles outside of town. They had no escort so we shot them all down. They didn't come back to Kunming for a year.

We had one guy we called Duke, who became an ace the first day. He shot down five Japanese bombers before another Japanese bomber shot everything off his airplane from the windscreen back. His airplane was totaled. A gunnery expert came up to him afterwards and asked him what special techniques he had used in the attack. "Well," Duke said, "you just drive up about 50 feet behind one of those Japanese airplanes, hold your trigger in until the damn thing drops, and then move along to the next one."

The first aircraft I shot down was a fighter. It was a small fighter with fixed landing gear and an open cockpit—

highly maneuverable but very flimsy. We were flying in Thailand, and we thought we were going to be a complete surprise, so we didn't bother to look up. Unfortunately, they had been alerted, and there were guys above us. I was so excited that I didn't even look through the gun sight. I pulled right up behind one…it just blew up. At that same time, one of the other airplanes made an overhead pass on me. He shot 33 holes in my plane, so I damn near bought the ranch. Then the next one came around at me head on, and I got him.

Action was pretty heavy during that time. The Japanese sent wave after wave of airplanes in. But we thinned them out. Finally, the Japanese ground forces came in, and we had to move. We went to the head of the Burma Road. Everything from there on had to move by truck.

We nearly got caught there. The Japanese were on their way when bad weather socked us in. We were beginning to wonder whether we would have to burn the airplanes and take off on foot when the ceiling raised to 800 feet, enabling us to sneak out. We still had to burn four airplanes because they were out of commission at the time we left.

A terrible thing happened at a little town on the way up the Burma Road. The roads were very primitive and all these refugees and their vehicles were backed up in one area. Some of our guys didn't have airplanes to fly, so they were driving trucks. The Japanese came in with bombers right in the middle of that congested area.

When the Japanese attacked, only one of our guys was able to get airborne. After he shot down their bomber, he thought that they were gone, so he came in and did a victory roll over the field. But there was a Zero right behind him, going right around with him. The Zero set him on fire. His face was badly burned, and a convoy doctor was taking care of him. Another of our crewmen had been hit in one of the trucks. His leg was blown off. Before the doctor could get to him, he was gone.

The original AVG "Flying Tigers" broke up in June 1942. Five pilots and 22 ground personnel volunteered to stay there to activate the new unit. After the group disbanded, I took a commission as major in the Army Air Corps. At the time I was still flying P-40s. Later we got P-51s.

Next I was moved up to group commander of the 23rd Fighter Group. One of the highlights of that time was a raid that I led on Formosa, on an airfield there. Our force was very small. We took everything that would make the trip. I had eight P-51s, ten P-38s, and 12 B-25s. We took off on the deck from a base in southeast China. It was highly secretive. If they had had early warning about our crossing, we would have lost everybody, because they had over 100 fighters on their field. We came in right on the deck, about 50 to 100 feet off the water.

When we approached the field, the bombers pulled up and dropped all the parafrags they were equipped with. We also caught some Japanese bombers that had been out on a mission somewhere. They were coming in for a landing. All the fuel trucks were on the field. You can't imagine the devastation. They got seven fighters airborne, but I shot down the first guy. All I had to do was raise my nose a little bit. I caught him almost head on. We strafed the field, and then headed back. We never lost anybody—never got a bullet hole. It was one of those perfect deals where you either lose everybody or lose nobody, and we didn't lose a one.

David Lee "Tex" Hill was a P-40 fighter pilot with the American Volunteer Group, "The Flying Tigers," 2nd Squadron. When the group disbanded in July 1942, he took a spot commission in the Army Air Corps and activated the 75th Fighter Squadron, 23rd Fighter Group. Credited with more than 18 aerial victories, Hill received six decorations from the Chinese government, the British Flying Cross, the Silver Star, three Distinguished Flying Crosses, two Air Medals, and the President's Distinguished Unit Citation.

February 1943 was when I went overseas and I returned before Thanksgiving of that same year, after flying approximately 50 missions. The first B-25 I flew was in Columbia, South Carolina. It had a great deal of power—acceleration was excellent, and it handled very nicely, so it was an easy airplane to fly and land, and it flew well on one engine.

The B-25 was a "dirty" airplane aerodynamically, so it handled well in formation. A dirty airplane is one that has a great deal of built-in drag. A stable aircraft, the B-25 will not pick up excessive speed, especially in a descent. It's much slower to accelerate when it gets out of the normal flight position.

The B-25 was a very sturdy aircraft, and it was highly maneuverable. We could do things in it that you just couldn't do in other bombers. There was an older B-25 that was kept at one of my bases. It was used mostly for ferrying supplies or ammunition. I remember guys taking that bomber up and dogfighting with the P-38s just for fun. And the airplane could sustain an awful lot of combat damage and still keep flying.

Formation depends on the type of aircraft, the number of planes going out on a mission, and the fields from which the planes are taking off. Our fields always had runways wide enough for three planes to take off together.

A formation of B-25s consisted of 12 planes from each squadron, three or four squadrons going out together. Planes rotated in the squadron group, so that one day you flew lead, the next day you flew number two, the following mission you flew number three, and so forth. The squadrons themselves would rotate the same way, one squadron leading one day, then falling into the number-two position the next time out.

I flew in a three-ship element within the 12-plane squadron. We had four elements of three planes each. The three-plane element would take off in formation, and then the next element would take off behind them. The first element slowed down once they cleared traffic so that the other elements could catch up with them. We formed very rapidly that way. Once airborne, we leveled off at about 500 feet. To avoid alerting enemy fighters, we remained at that low altitude until we got a certain distance from the target area, each plane flying at a slightly lower altitude. You used the reference points on the plane in front of you to hold your position in formation.

We were hard on our engines, and they had to be changed frequently. Sometimes an engine only ran for 100 hours. We flew on and off dirt fields, so it was very dusty, and dust wore out the engines. On takeoff an element kicked up a lot of dirt, which meant the next element had to wait for the dust to settle a little before it could take off.

Two or three extra planes always followed the formation, flying slightly above us, ready to fill in if somebody had mechanical problems. In the air we test-fired all our guns to make sure everything worked. If a pilot experienced problems with the guns or with over-heating engines, he would drop out of formation, and one of the spares would take his place. Most of our missions were conducted over the Mediterranean. We flew in a formation where the last three-plane element was literally skimming the water. The power and stability of the B-25 made this possible. None of the B-25 manuals ever came close to being accurate, with respect to power settings and fuel consumption. The airplane was much faster and stronger than the manuals claimed.

On a mission, we'd start gaining altitude in time to be about 1,000 feet above the "Initial Point." The IP was an easily distinguishable place on the ground about 10 miles from the target. When we reached the IP, we started our final climb to about 1,000 feet above bombing altitude, which was normally 6,500 feet above the terrain.

We didn't like it there, and we took violent evasive action to avoid anti-aircraft fire. When we got near anti-aircraft fire, we always spread out so that if a plane was hit, we wouldn't fly into the debris. Violent evasive action meant going up and down better than 500 feet and making 90-degree turns. At times we'd even put the entire formation into a 90-degree bank, stabilize at the IP, and make a run at the target.

As soon as the lead ship dropped its bombs, the bombardiers on the other planes dropped theirs. We usually conducted area bombing, although sometimes our mission was to hit a bridge or railroad tracks. On those assignments, we would fly at a slight angle to the target in order to get the bombs to drop across them and do as much damage as possible. Most targets were over Sicily, and they were strategic rather than tactical targets, meaning we did not directly support ground troops.

As long as you were busy flying, it wasn't quite as unnerving to see fighters coming at you or to watch explosions around you. However, you knew you were much too close to an explosion if you saw red instead of black. Going into a target, we'd stabilize, and as soon as the bombadier said, "Bombs away!" and "Doors closed!" we got the hell out of there.

Our bombing was extremely accurate, because having taken violent evasion action on the way into the target area, we weren't so scared that we couldn't hold the ship in good bombing runs. We had no problem hitting a target.

The airspeed indicator in the B-25 had a red line at 360, but we seldom came off a target with a reading of less than 450, which meant we could get to the Italian coastline rather quickly, to say the least. We liked that. We weren't heroes. Enemy fighters won't come after you when you're in tight formation over the water.

German tactics were identical to ours. Their fighters attacked bomber formations by starting from above. Their planes were protected by armor plate on the bottom, so they'd roll over upside down, make a pass from above, fire as they were going past, and then get out of there. It was called a "split S" move. They couldn't do that maneuver, though, once we were down over the water. There was no room to recover after the dive past, and if you have 48 planes with guns pointing at you, you're not going to come in head on.

Enemy fighters left us alone once the anti-aircraft guns started firing, but when they started putting up shells with colored bursts, that indicated that they were going to stop firing from the ground. Then the fighters would come back in. Usually, P-38s escorted us, because of their speed and maneuverability. They did an excellent job protecting us, so we didn't have much trouble with enemy fighters. A couple of times we had Spitfire escorts, but they couldn't stay with us because they didn't have the range. The A-36, which was an early version of the P-51, tried to escort us, but it couldn't keep up with us either. We'd make a rapid climb to the target at our cruising speed and leave everybody behind.

A B-25 would carry any kind of load that you put on it. We loaded ours with armor plate—up the sides of the bows, a piece that came slightly over our heads, another under our legs and rudder pedals. The B-25 had been designed with a little piece of armor up the back of the seat, but that wasn't worth much to us, so we added our own.

We had some difficult missions along the west coast of

Italy. The mountains come down close to the Mediterranean there, and railroad tracks were located in a narrow area between the mountains and the water. We flew a number of missions over these railroad tracks, trying to stop supplies from getting through.

One time we were supposed to hit a railroad located about 75 miles south of Rome, but instead of winding up at our Initial Point before the final run, we wound up in Rome itself. We got out of there in a hurry and finally made it to our target, but it was clear that our navigator had screwed up.

We flew several difficult missions over Sicily, where we were so low that anti-aircraft guns mounted on the sides of Mt. Aetna were actually shooting down at us. There's not much evasive action you can take in that situation.

As a pilot hauling a bomber around, you're exerting a good bit of energy. It's not like flying a fighter plane. When you haul back on the B-25's control column at 300 mph, it's brutal. You're flying off the wing of another plane, and you're trying to keep from running into him, so you don't have time to worry about the flak and the fighters. We were able to make a brief bombing run of about 15 to 20 seconds without being so scared that we couldn't hold it in position. And we could hold it very accurately.

I received holes in the windshield and various other parts of my airplane, but no crew member of mine was ever injured. Our group had very low losses. A couple of men went down in the waters off Sicily, but they were picked up by amphibious air-sea rescue planes. Our Navy was out there all the time, too. Even partisans on the ground would send out rowboats for us. The Germans weren't popular with anyone over there at that time.

Our group flew three missions one day against a fighter base on Pantelleria Island off the coast of Africa. The place was occupied by Italians. As soon as our bomb-bay doors opened, the anti-aircraft fire would stop until we closed our doors again. We bombed the heck out of it but did little

damage, because the place was solid rock. The enemy's gunnery emplacements were cut into the rock, and their aircraft were in caves. The only way we could have done much damage was to slide a bomb in through the door, but I don't think anyone ever managed that.

Probably the happiest people in Africa were our Italian prisoners, because they were out of the war and had good clothing and food. They were our cooks, and they even worked on our jeeps, getting them in excellent condition. When it was time for them to leave us, they didn't want to go.

We had British rations once or twice, but normally, we ate C-rations. There were three different combinations— meat and vegetable stew, meat and vegetable hash, and meat and beans. In another can you'd get powdered coffee, lemonade, or cocoa. The coffee never tasted any good, because the water needed to make it had chlorine in it. If you tried making coffee, you only managed to stink up your tent. Everybody always wanted the cocoa instead. About all we could do for recreation was play poker. The house rules were that you could play until you lost $20 or until midnight, whichever came first.

Philip O. Carr flew B-25 Mitchell bombers with the 446th Squadron, 321st Bombardment Group (Medium), 14th Army Air Force. He was credited with 50 combat missions and was awarded the Air Medal with ten Oak Leaf Clusters.

From the time I was five years old, I wanted to fly airplanes. Back in the '30s you needed at least two years of college to apply to either the Navy Air Force or the Army Air Force. So after I had gotten my two years in, I applied to the Navy.

I was turned down because of something called the Snyder test, a respiratory test where the doctor takes your pulse. I wanted to fly so badly, every time I took that test, my pulse would just start racing. For two and a half years, I tried all around—Pensacola, Panama City, San Antonio—to pass that test, and every time, my pulse would jump up to about 140.

Finally, an old Navy doctor said, "I'm going to give you a chance, son," and he wrote up a passing Snyder, along with a letter for the base doctor. In training I managed to graduate in the top ten percent of my class, which enabled me to volunteer for the Marine Corps. This was just before the bombing of Pearl Harbor.

I went overseas on a deluxe passenger liner to Honolulu and from there on a ship to New Caledonia. It was a long trip through submarine-infested areas. Most of the time only one engine worked. The ship was a German transport that had been sunk, beached, and salvaged by the Allies. The Germans had used it for "propagation" purposes, where unmarried men and women were sent out on cruises and introduced to each other.

After I reached New Caledonia, I was flown into Guadalcanal on a DC-3. The first thing my commanding officer did when I arrived was put me into an F4F Wildcat fighter, and I flew a patrol to acclimate myself to the controls.

When I first got in the Wildcat, I didn't fully appreciate the aircraft. To me it wasn't as agile as the Brewster Buffaloes I had flown before back in the States, but it had an engine that could stand anything. You could run it wide open until it was out of fuel. Those engines were marvelous.

The Wildcat was tough, too. I had a friend who had gotten loose on a flight and was heading back home by himself when three Zeroes attacked him. His airplane was riddled with holes, but they never got him. The armor plate had saved him. Now, if a Japanese plane was shot down, it meant that the Japanese lost both an airplane and a pilot. Their aircraft didn't have heavy armor plate or self-sealing tanks, so they didn't have the strength to stay together if they were hit several times in combat. There were good Zero pilots, but we shot them down with F4Fs almost five-to-one.

I remember that when we left the States, they told us that Zeroes were far superior to our own fighters. But after we got to Guadalcanal, a man there told us that everything we had heard about Zeroes back home was horseshit. Our instructors had told us to get above the Zeroes, make a pass, and retire. But this pilot said that the Zeroes weren't stressed for heavy engagement. He said their airplanes were death traps if they were hit, so we should get close, get our noses on them, and use the six guns. And we shot down airplanes that way.

One day I crossed through a storm to intercept nine Zeroes that were making passes at an eight-plane flight of

our own up ahead of me. Unfortunately, once I got through the storm, I found out that I had lost the rest of my own flight, so I ended up cornering the Zeroes all by myself. They didn't even realize I was there. I got two of them pretty quick before the rest of the Jap planes were all around me. They knocked my engine out so that I couldn't use my power, and it was shaking the airplane to pieces. I just dived out from 20,000 feet because I knew they couldn't stay with me.

At 20,000 feet nothing performed like the Corsair. Every fight that I ever started was in the 15,000 to 25,000-foot range. I shot down nine enemy aircraft at Guadalcanal—eight of them in a Corsair. In the Corsair you sit in a big seat in the back, and of course, that's a tremendous advantage in combat. The tank is between the engine and the pilot, and it is protected by bomber plate and the pilot's armor. As a gun platform the aircraft is absolutely peerless.

On high combat-patrol we wore warm clothes, but the aircraft was well sealed, and the canopy was closed. Plus there was heat from the sun, so the cold never really bothered us at the 20,000-foot level.

Since the Japs would come in high, our patrols were at 30,000 feet. Up there it is absolute North Pole weather. It's pure ice. If you hit a cloud, it's already frozen. I used to fly top-cover patrols where I'd get so cold that after I came aboard the carrier, it would be 30 minutes before I warmed up. Of course, the cold also made landing more difficult, because you were so stiff. We never stayed on high patrol beyond two hours.

Searches, though, might last up to six hours. Since it wasn't an attack mission, you carried defensive weapons—drop tanks and six 50-caliber guns, for instance. I remember flying a search to Iwo Jima one day. We were looking for anything hostile in that area, and we nearly ran aground because the ceiling was so low. Although we had radar, cloud cover was a problem. As we let down through the clouds returning to the carrier from a mission, one of my men hit the mast of a cruiser with his airplane. We looked him over and didn't see any damage. But when he started aboard, the landing officer gave him the cut. He had lost his tailhook on the mast of the cruiser! Just the hook. And he hit the barrier.

They once gave me 43 pilots to train, out of which only 28 qualified. Some of those guys who didn't make it might have been good in combat, but they couldn't handle the carrier part. We began training them in the desert, and when you land in the desert and catch a hook, you're going just a little faster than you are when you are on a carrier. You couldn't look, you just had to believe that the hook was there, because the taxi operation was critical. You had only 20 seconds to disengage, get out of the way, get the wings folded, and go.

A Marine pilot never had his own airplane, the commanding officer included. If you were a leader, you got the front plane, whether it was No. 16 or No. 32. No one could count on having any particular aircraft. Of course, I don't recall any airplanes on deck that weren't in prime condition.

On one mission I was escorting some torpedo bombers in an F4F. We were on our way to finish off a Japanese battleship that was crippled with a bad rudder. The night before, the Japs had gone right down the strip, knocking off our planes from battleships and cruisers. There were only seven fighters left on Guadalcanal because of what they'd done the night before.

It was on that mission that I shot down my first airplane. On our way to the battleship I noticed Japs flying over us, but even though I had only three fighters, just one of those nine Japanese planes made a pass at the bombers. I moved over, blew him up, and came back. That was all. The other Japanese airplanes left us alone, so we went out and attacked their battleship. I never have understood it, why they didn't hit us.

My wingman was a guy named "Butterball" Webb. One time we were in a big air fight. I had shot down four airplanes and thought that no more were coming, but old Butterball said over the radio, "Someone come get this guy. My guns are jammed." I looked down to my left and saw Butterball right on a Jap's tail. He was trying to cut his rudder with the Corsair's prop. Just like I did the time I got my

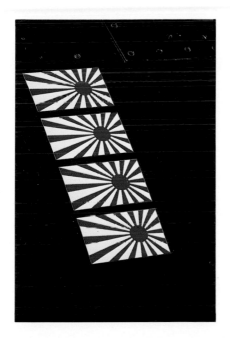

first plane, I dropped down, moved over, blew him up, and rejoined the formation.

Then old Butterball joined up with me. All of a sudden I heard a lot of ammunition going by. It was from Butterball's plane. His guns hadn't been jammed. He just hadn't turned them on. I realized that he had done that on purpose so that I could get that second ace.

Even though I made an ace one day in Guadalcanal, and an ace in a day at Okinawa, when you're out after surface ships, your skill doesn't matter as much. Attacking an armed surface ship is the most dangerous thing in the world because you can't dodge their fire. How do you dodge when a bunch of ships are shooting at you? You don't have any

idea of what to do except go in, make your pass, and retire. We would try to deflect their shots by coming in and bothering the gunners that were shooting our torpedo bombers.

Of course, no matter what anyone tells you, you can't remember a whole fight—it just happens too fast. Once you get 20 or 30 aircraft in the air, it's hard to tell exactly what takes place. Something flashes by, and you realize it's the enemy, so you get an opportunity. You go in, do it, and get out.

Mornings often brought the kamikazes. Sometimes they would come in and start for the *Bunker Hill,* but there was so much firepower from our ship that they'd swing over and go to another one. The *Bunker Hill* was Admiral Mitscher's flagship, and it was the most protected ship in the fleet. We used to stand on deck and say that it was as safe to be there as it was to be in a church in Iowa.

But one time the kamikazes did hit us. I had been leading a flight of 16 planes—I think it was over Okinawa. Our flight was cancelled, so we came in for debriefing. The kamikazes apparently followed our shadow in, because the radar never picked them up. Within 30 seconds of each other, two kamikaze pilots flew in and hit the *Bunker Hill.* There were a lot of airplanes on deck at the time. In fact, they had all been respotted for takeoff. The next thing I knew there was a fire raging in the hangar and a fire raging on deck. The ready rooms between those two places became an oven. That attack put the *Bunker Hill* out of action for the rest of the war.

Archie Donahue, a Marine Corps pilot, was first assigned to VMF-112, flying F4F-4 Wildcats and F4U-1 Corsairs, and was later assigned to VMF-451. He flew a total of 215 combat missions and is credited with 14 confirmed aerial victories. He was decorated with the Navy Cross, three Distinguished Flying Crosses, and five Air Medals.

On my 18th birthday I signed up with the Navy as a Seaman Second Class, determined to become a pilot. They had changed the regulations, so you could become a pilot without having had any college.

I don't know why I decided on flying. Probably it was the glamour of it. I'd always been intrigued by airplanes, even though I'd never flown one. There was a certain excitement to it. And I always had great respect for the Navy, for its excellence—I remember going aboard a destroyer docked in New York City in 1939 and being very impressed. At any rate, when I was very, very young, I decided that I wanted to be a Navy pilot, a carrier-based Navy pilot.

But I guess the real reason I enlisted was that our country had been bombed six months before at Pearl Harbor, and when June of '42 rolled around and I graduated from my boarding school, I wanted to go out and fight for freedom, and against the Imperialist Nazis, like most young men of the time. It wasn't a hard decision.

My pre-flight training took place at Chapel Hill, North Carolina, and the first time I ever flew was in Minneapolis, Minnesota. They started us flying those yellow, two-winged, open-cockpit trainers. We flew in the coldest weather you can imagine. I never landed without snow and ice on the ground until I got to Corpus Christi, Texas, and some outlying airbases near Corpus, for advanced training.

After I got my wings at Corpus, I went through torpedo-bomber training. Our group was assigned to the U.S.S. *San Jacinto,* my first and only ship. We put her into commission and went on a shakedown cruise to Trinidad, then went on around through the Panama Canal and out into the Pacific in early 1944.

Boredom was a part of many of the day-to-day missions. We did a lot of what was called "ASP"—antisubmarine patrol. We'd go out in front of the fleet—each torpedo-bomber pilot being assigned a certain sector, and we'd search visually for submarines or for hostile military action of any kind on the part of the Japanese. Fighters provided cover for us up top. We spent hours searching open water, with very infrequent sightings.

Most of the actual combat situations in the TBM Avenger were glide-bombing missions. You'd push your plane over in a 35-degree angle, and release 400- or 500-pound bombs at the target. That was the kind of mission I was on the day I got shot down.

My target was a radio station near the island of Iwo Jima. We came in high, up about 10-12,000 feet. The air was full of very black, ominous puffs that seemed almost surrealistic. I'd been shot at before, but never anything quite this

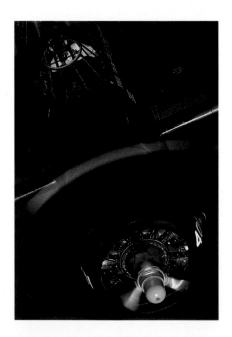

intense. You couldn't hear the bursts, but you could almost feel the puffs of black smoke around you from anti-aircraft gunfire that was coming up from the ground.

A few minutes later, I was hit about halfway down my bombing run. My plane caught on fire, and the cockpit filled up with smoke. I continued the run and released my bombs over the target. This was all split-second stuff—not fast by today's standards, but red-line by old standards. I released

the bombs, pulled out to sea, and then realized that my airplane was simply not flyable.

The wings on a torpedo bomber fold, and the gas tanks are on either side of the seam. There was a fire right along the fold of the wings, which made me think that at any minute the wing tanks would blow. I could hardly see the instruments because smoke had filled the compartment. There were two men in the back of the Avenger, so I put the plane in a right-hand turn—standard bail-out procedure—so the men could get out the door in the back. One of them did bail out, but his parachute failed to open, so he was killed. The other man was probably hit by gunfire, because he never made it out.

After I made a full 360-degree turn, I radioed our skipper, put the airplane into a turn, and bailed out myself. If you went out, you hopefully did it better than I did. The TBM had a bar across the top of it. You were supposed to hoist yourself out by the bar and then dive out onto the wing, but I pulled the rip cord too early. My head struck the tail of the plane so hard that I thought I had been wounded. As a matter of fact, another torpedo-bomber pilot saw me and dropped some medical supplies because he thought I'd been really hurt. Actually, it was like the strawberry that you get when you slide on your side in baseball. It took the skin off the whole side of my face, but there was no other damage at all.

The Avenger wasn't a plane that was easy to get out of—you couldn't dump it upside down because of that bar crossing on top of your head. But I'm not too proud of my exit from the airplane.

After bailing out, I landed in the Pacific fairly close to a Japanese-held island. I'm sure that I broke the standing record for the 100-yard swimming dash to get my life raft and paddle out to sea. We had been briefed earlier on the fact that this was the last day our carrier was going to be in northern Pacific waters. That night, Mitscher's Fifth Fleet was going to turn into Halsey's Third Fleet and set sail for the general area of the Philippines. I knew that somebody had better pick me up that night or I would be picked up by the Japanese, and indeed, they did send a boat out, but it was strafed.

Because rescue submarines were stationed nearby as often as possible when we made raids like this, I knew there was a submarine on patrol. In fact, there was a special code to call when we got in distress, which I had called. The trouble is you never knew if the submarine had gotten the message. So I must say, I was apprehensive. I didn't know what was going to happen for a couple of hours, and then out of the sea came a periscope and then a submarine, and I'm glad it turned out to be ours.

I'd been on the deck of a submarine before, but I'd never been on a patrol. I stayed aboard for about 30 days. To get air, we went topside and stood watch at night. Those were some of the most majestic nights I've ever seen in my life—stars so bright, you could touch them.

The submarine's commanding officer was aggressive. In fact, he was awarded the Silver Star for the amount of Japanese tonnage sunk while I was right there on board. We got depth-charged a lot, so it was more terrifying than flying. The submariners didn't think so, but we three pilots that were picked up did.

The submarine didn't have any extra beds, so when one guy climbed out of bed, I climbed in. It was dank in there, too, because the air conditioning wasn't so good. You could take a shower once a week, and even then some guy would be standing there with a stopwatch seeing that you didn't use up more than 20 seconds worth of water.

The submarine took me back to Midway, where I hitched a ride down to Pearl Harbor. I had some rest time there, and then I hitchhiked back to the fleet, which was thousands of miles away by that time out in the Philippines. The last air strike I flew was over Manila in the Philippine

Islands. Then we were released in time for Christmas '44. After the holiday, I joined another squadron—had our orders to go out overseas again—but the war ended. In the meantime I'd been married, so I was thrilled about all that.

I liked the Avenger because it was stable, had a large wing. It was then the biggest, single-engine plane, I believe, in either the Army Air Corps or the Navy. The beautiful thing about the airplane was its ability to land on a tossing deck. Our carrier was a fast carrier, but it had a very narrow hull, so the Avenger was reassuring. You could settle that airplane down and not worry as much about spinning in like you could with a Corsair or an F6F Hellcat. The Avenger was also dependable. You could take a hit, and the plane would still fly.

It was also watertight. One time my plane was having engine trouble, and the ship couldn't take me on board, so I had to land in the water, loaded with two men and 400- or 500-pound depth charges. There was a little bit of sea at the time. I landed tail first, and the hull came in next. Once the plane was in the water, I climbed out onto the wing, and my crewmen climbed out through the turret. Amazingly, no one had gotten wet. We pulled out the life raft and then watched the plane float for a while before it gradually sank to the depths of the Pacific.

My Navy experience was the single most maturing experience I had. I went in as an 18-year-old kid out of a rather sheltered environment, and I came out having nearly lost my life a couple of times.

I saw sights right on our flight deck. I had just landed my plane once, and I saw a guy cut in half. The flight deck was stunned, but our fantastic chief petty officer yelled at the men, "Grab a hose. Clean this mess up. Come on, let's get this ship flying." It was a life lost, and then it was life going on. All this made an impression on me as a 19- and 20-year-old kid. It really formed my impressions about the need for a strong military, the need for our country to be together when things get rough out there. I hope combat is something none of my five kids or nine grandchildren will ever be involved in, but it's given my life a dimension that I wouldn't have gotten otherwise. And it's given me a great respect for the armed services of the United States.

Today, it doesn't seem like it all happened, and yet, it's been a very internal and important part of my life. The saddest part has been the loss of those two crewmen who were depending on me for their lives.

George H. Bush flew a TBM Avenger in the Navy's VT-51 Torpedo Bomber Squadron based on the U.S.S. San Jacinto. Commissioned as an ensign, he received his wings before his 19th birthday, making him the youngest pilot in the Navy. Bush logged 126 carrier landings, flew 58 missions, and received the Distinguished Flying Cross and three Air Medals.

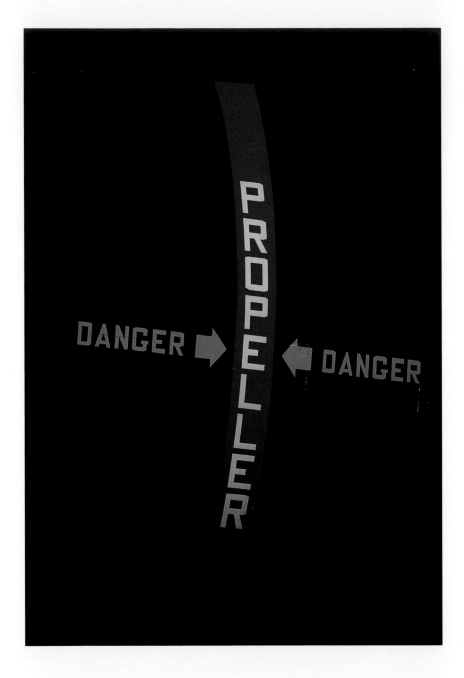

COMBAT CAMERAMEN, TECHNICAL TRAINING SCHOOL

Negotiations with Japan appear to be terminated to all practical purposes with only barest possibilities that Japanese Government might come back and offer to continue. Japanese future action unpredictable but hostile action possible at any moment. If hostilities cannot, repeat cannot, be avoided, the U.S. desires that Japan commit the first overt act.

—message from General George C. Marshall to General Douglas MacArthur, 27 November 1941

HEAVY-BOMBER AIR CREW

(For physical inspection) we would bend
over in front of one medical officer while
another would look down our throats. If they
didn't see each other, they would hand us a
bible, and we were "in."

—personal account

The last mile, the mile from the squadron area to the railroad station, found the...Group saying farewell to Charleston and thus to the United States as we boarded the train that was to take us to Camp Patrick Henry (Virginia), to Port of Embarkation, to War. With full field pack and arms, we passed in review...and turned toward the siding that held the waiting cars for our last major troop movement in the United States. We marched in silence, none of us thinking of the songs we used to sing while marching in basic training. We didn't feel like singing—someone murmured: Well, this is it!

...For an hour we were to ride a train once more. This was the short trip from Camp Patrick Henry to the docks where three United States Army Transports, little Liberty ships, waited to carry...(us) overseas. ...Now that we were going, an emotional strain and nervous tension could be read in each of our faces as we climbed into the crowded coaches. Through the dirty windows of the coaches we caught a few last glimpses of America....

—PERSONAL ACCOUNT

AT-6 TEXANS

FEBRUARY 14, 1944. Valentine's Day...Briefing before mission was held in a wine cellar under Headquarters Building. Had big map at one end of the building with spot light on map. Chaplain opened session with prayer. Map at end of room was covered with large window shade. Shade was raised after prayer so we could see exactly where we were going. Intelligence officers and weather officers gave their reports. We then knew what kind of anti-aircraft was on the ground, how long they would shoot at us during our pass over the target; how many fighters were in the area and what kind of trouble we could expect from them. We were also told what kind of fighter protection we would have from American bases and where they would meet us.

—PERSONAL DIARY

FEBRUARY 14, 1944. After six hours with no food, during the mission, we were met at the plane when we landed by the Medical Officer and if we wanted a "shot" (2 oz.) of whiskey, he was there to give it to us. From this point we went back to the wine cellar for debriefing. Don't know how intelligent our report of mission was—the whiskey hit some kind of hard!

—PERSONAL DIARY

FEBRUARY 17, 1944. GOT CABLE TODAY THAT MY SON WAS BORN FEBRUARY 13, 1944!

—personal diary

B-17 FLYING FORTRESSES

B-17 FLYING FORTRESS

Second or third mission, (tailgunner) Jim Fisher
froze his hands and his oxygen mask didn't fit right.
His eyebrows were white with frost. A mission where
the temperature went to 54 degrees below zero.

—personal diary, February 1944

After a bomb run, the bomb-bay door became jammed by shell cases from the upper local turret. Kirby tried to use the bomb-bay door activating handle under the flight deck. This wouldn't work, and the open doors were slowing us up; we might lose the formation. I started to move forward on the cat-walk from the tail. Because the doors were open, I snapped one hook of the chest parachute into place and filled an oxygen walk around bottle. It was impossible to fit between the bomb racks wearing this equipment. Both the chest pack and the oxygen bottle were left in the rear. With one foot on the cat-walk and holding on to a bomb rack with one hand and some tubing with the other (the tubing was on the far side of the bomb-bay), I tried to kick the 50-calibre shell cases out of the door track. One or two of the shell cases could not be budged. During this time, Kirby had periodically tried to use the activating bomb door handle under the flight deck in an attempt to either fully open or close the doors. The doors remained jammed in a position that would be about 2 feet toward a closed position. This left the door open approximately 3½ ft. You were never to stand on the bomb-bay doors, but the only way to get this situation cleared up was to bend over and jiggle the shell cases loose by hand. In order to do this, I had to put one foot on the bomb-bay door across the open area. Luckily, I was able to free the shell cases. Kirby thought I had already taken my weight off the bomb-bay door and activated the control valve to open position. I did not have to tell my feet what to do, it was discovered they had a mind of their own and they got me back to the cat-walk. Kirby was as white as I when he realized what had happened. The doors were then fully closed and we regained our position in the group.

—PERSONAL DIARY, 1944

WAIST-GUNNER, B-24 LIBERATOR

P-39 AIRACOBRA

6/26/44. This was a very exciting mission. Everything went along swell until we were about thirty minutes from the target and then all hell broke loose. I never saw so many fighters in all my life as I saw today. We had one group of P-38 escorts and one group of P-51's but needed twice as many. The fighters did a marvelous job keeping most of the Jerries busy and shot down dozens of planes. A lot of our B-24's went down too. Lost three out of our group. I got in a couple of good shots but didn't score one. The Jerries sent up around thirty two-engine fighters which attacked in one pack. I never felt so helpless in all my life than I did when the two-engines made their attack. I watched a very large dogfight between our fighters and the Jerries' single-engine fighters. Planes were blowing up and going down like flies. I just hope and pray that they were all enemy planes.

—PERSONAL DIARY

P-51 MUSTANG

P-38 LIGHTNINGS

Popular movies included "Thunderbirds," starring Gene Tierny, and "Navy Blues," starring Ann Sheridan. Dancers and romancers enjoyed the popular songs "Begin the Beguine" by Artie Shaw, "Deep Purple" by Tommy Dorsey, and Glenn Miller's "In the Mood."

P-47 THUNDERBOLTS

171

APRIL 12, 1944. Another big raid—way up into Austria proper. Flew over Austrian Alps, still snow capped, to hit our target, Bad Voslau—an aircraft factory. We were routed to fly right through the flak. We missed the flak, but the ME-110's, JU-88's, ME-109's and FW-190's jumped us right over the target. We got our ship shot up pretty badly. This was the first mission for our new tail gunner and he got hit in the shoulder by a piece of 20mm shell. He had not fired a round yet—only test fired. Most of the tail end of our ship was shot up—but it got us home. I got two big holes (6 to 8 inches each) in my top turret and got a hole in Peyton's (pilot) window. Really, there were holes all over the whole ship. I shot almost all my ammo—everyone did. One JU-88 followed us almost all the way back and kept making passes at us. We saw a B-24 go down and 9 or 10 chutes opened from it. Our engines really caught hell—#1 is the only one that survived the trip...#2 got hit, supercharger shot out and wing hit bad...Lost #3—some mechanical difficulty, of all things...#4 got the carburetor lines shot off of it. We also got some big ones in the wings and another hit on our elevator that screwed up the tabs. I could have stopped the #4 running wild by shutting off the gas line, but we needed its power to bring us home. It was hung at top speed....

We dumped all of our ammo, machine guns and waist guns—and everything we could get loose and that did not pertain to the actual flying of the ship it went into the Adriatic Sea. If #4 had quit on us, we'd have one and a half engines left and it takes a good healthy two of them to keep that baby in the air. (It took the ground crew a full four weeks to put the plane back together in flying condition....)

Air time was 0900 to 1455 hours—in that six hours a whole lifetime passed before us....

—PERSONAL DIARY

GROUND CREW AND ORDNANCE

B-25 MITCHELL

We were hit by twin-engine German fighters. They sprayed the formation with 20mm cannon and were out of range of our 50-cal. guns most of the time. Lewis had about 80% of tail turret blown up around him. Part of the shell ripped out his oxygen regulator right next to his left shoulder and also cut the electrical wiring to the turret. There was a cloud of blue-grey smoke in the tail and for this reason, we believe it was an explosive shell. We also heard a loud report. Lewis did not answer calls on the inter-com and I proceeded back to the tail turret. To this day, I do not know if he was aware of the fact that I was in back of him, but he fell into my arms just as I reached him. He was pulled out of the turret in a dazed condition and complained of his shoulder hurting. It was too cold to remove his clothing, so I put my hand inside his outer-garments to his underwear. When I withdrew my hand, there was no blood on it, and Lewis was sent to the flight deck to regain his composure. I got into the tail turret and found that the guns would not fire; however, it was possible to move the turret manually, so I stayed there because moving guns would indicate to the fighters that the position was still manned. Someone of the crew kept me supplied with refilled walk-around oxygen bottles.

—PERSONAL DIARY, 12 APRIL 1944

NOSE-GUNNER, B-24 LIBERATOR

B-17 FLYING FORTRESSES

APRIL 29, 1944. Went to Toulon, France, where the target was a munitions plant. Boy, what a lot of flak...red, white, black puffs all around us. We only got one little hole in the ship. We had no fighters attack us, though we saw a few fighters attack another bomb group. They put up enough flak for us to walk on, but it was short of our altitude. The red bursts appeared as we were leaving the target. We think that this was the anti-aircraft gunners way of telling the fighters that they were ceasing fire, and that it was up to them to pursue us if they were going to. This also told their fighter pilots that they could dive through our formations without the fear of being hit by their own flak.

—PERSONAL DIARY

BALL TURRET, B-17 FLYING FORTRESS

177

MAY 18, 1944. Ploesti, Romania. All of us ran short of gas..."Coming in on a wing and a prayer" really means something after one of these runs. We saw several P-38's ditch their planes because they were out of gas and our bombers flew circles around them and dropped life rafts to them—in the Adriatic—and radioed their position to the Air-Sea Rescue. Eleven planes had to land at Bari, Italy, because of gas shortage. We shot flares at our home base to be given priority to land, because we knew our gas supply was all but gone. As we taxied to our revetment one engine stopped—dry well, and as we turned around to park on the revetment, another engine quit on us.

—PERSONAL DIARY

B-24 LIBERATORS

B-24 LIBERATOR

They have a public address system throughout the barracks and they play a recording of reveille. This is immediately followed by a full-volume blast of Benny Goodman's "Idaho." If we are not out of bed by then, they follow with some Harlem maniacs' recording of "Cow Boogie."

—PERSONAL ACCOUNT

In February of 1944, the Allied Armies in Italy were still being held at Cassino in what was to become one of the toughest campaigns of World War II. At the same time, Allied troops captured Solomon and Caroline Islands, while the Japs continued a drive through Burma to overrun British positions. During this month, Japan announced that her draft had been extended to include all men from the ages of twelve to sixty. And back in the States headlines were made by congressmen bickering over whether or not the soldier should vote in the coming elections, and by Charlie Chaplin who was charged by Joan Barry as being the father of her illegitimate child.

B-25 MITCHELL

HQS. WESTERN DESERT AIR FORCE, 19 February 1943. Keen rivalry existed among the three squadrons of the 57th Fighter Group: the "Fighting Cocks," so called because they brought a gamecock mascot with them from the States; the "Black Scorpions," who got their name when a sergeant found one of the deadly spiders in his bedroll; and the "Exterminators," whose name evolved from Squadron X. The 57th was full of fun as well as fight. Once I saw a "Keep off the Grass" sign on a plot of desert sand ten feet square that they had roped off. Another one of their sign posts was: "Los Angeles City Limits."

—General Lewis H. Brereton

B-24 BASE, ITALY

The enlisted men had many ingenious innovations in their tent; the table and chairs were made of bomb fin crates; the door, of two ½ gallon tin bacon cans with a plexiglas window; the ice-box of K-ration crates; individual closets from fragmentation bomb crates; a stove that had a heart of a German 88mm shell case and the outside was a cut-down 50-gallon gas drum; the frying pan was made of a 5-gallon oil can with a piece of angle iron welded to it for a handle. Our beds (Army cots) were balanced on six one-gallon tin cans in order to prevent the lizards from coming in out of the cold.

—PERSONAL DIARY, 1944

B-24 LIBERATORS

GENTLEMEN, A TOAST

When I return from Italy with mud upon my feet,

With mud upon my pants and shirt, mud in every pleat,

With mud beneath my fingernails, mud all through my hair,

I'll step into the nearest bar and climb upon a chair;

Then I'll announce to all the world: I've mud inside me, too,

And since I have to wash it out, the drinks are all on you;

But let me warn you 'fore you start, I'll shoot the first damn guy

Who raises up his glass and toasts, "Well, here's mud in your eye."

"Inner Sanctum" played on radio in 1944, its fourth consecutive year on the air. The show featured macabre scripts and creepy scenarios.

CHUNGKING, CHINA, 13 June 1942. (Chennault) was completely responsible for development of the tactics which enabled the Flying Tigers, using slower and inferior P-40s, to outperform the best Jap Zeros. Chennault devised the "hit and run" tactics and thoroughly imbued his pilots against the idea of engaging in prolonged dog-fights with the Japs. The Japs feared him as much as any man in the Far East and put a price on his head, dead or alive. Deaf as a post, Chennault would sit around in conferences like a cigar-store Indian. However, he was a good lip-reader and his agile mind followed everything closely.…Although he had a reputation for being damned tough, he had a fatherly way with his men. They all loved him.

—GENERAL LEWIS H. BRERETON

P-40 WARHAWK

B-17 FLYING FORTRESS

MAY 14, 1944. We took off at 0920, the target was Piacenza Airdrome at San Desenzano, Italy. We had 240 fragmentary bombs aboard. We encountered no flak nor fighters at the target, but came within from two to five feet of getting much worse. Our own B-17's were 2,000 feet overhead—right over our formation and were dropping their payload One of the bombs passed right between our engines #3 and #4...another barely missed the waist gun by 2 feet. Boy, all of us were really praying.

—PERSONAL DIARY

C-46 COMMANDO

We were pretty bewildered most of the time because we wanted to fly, and we got madder and madder the more the Japs raided Clark Field (Philippines), which was often. After the first attack, living conditions were pretty bad. We lived in nipa shacks (made out of reeds) or in rifle butts. We didn't have any tents. These places were something like dugouts, and we did all our cooking, sleeping, and everything there. No one ever took a bath. I don't think any of us changed clothes during the first week. Everything was filthy. Everything was covered with dust, and the filth hurt our morale worse than the Japs did.

—LIEUTENANT PETE BENDER, DECEMBER 1941

The Greyhound Bus System not only turned their transportation capabilities into a war effort, they made a technicolor film entitled, "This Amazing America," to help satisfy soldiers homesick for another glimpse of their homeland. The film is a pictorial journey across America. It was shown at outposts, in hospitals, on transports, and before battles to boost morale.

I have been looking at a list of the War Department contracts being filled here in Southern California. It takes three closely typed pages. Those of you who actually make airplanes can see where *you* come in, all right. A few more planes—or even one more plane in some cases—may make a real difference in the outcome of a mission.

It is a little harder, if you spend all day making turnbuckles or valves or rheostats. I can only tell you that we have got to have them, as many as you can make, as fast as you can make them. That is your part and I know you are going to do it.

—SPEECH BY GENERAL HENRY H. ARNOLD, 30 DECEMBER 1943

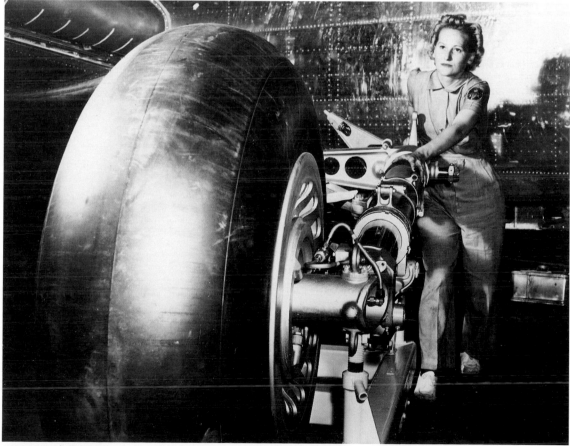

AIRCRAFT MANUFACTURE

February 1945—While the historic invasion of Iwo Jima was beginning, at home Bing Crosby's upbeat tune, "Accentuate the Positive" was heard on radio stations and Bennett Cerf's humorous <u>Try and Stop Me</u> was popular.

F6F HELLCATS

B-25 MITCHELL

192

THE EYES OF THE ENTIRE WORLD FRIEND AND ENEMY ARE FOCUSED IN ADMIRATION UPON THE OFFICERS AND MEN OF THE AMERICAN AIR FORCES IN THE PHILIPPINES. THE FIGHTING SPIRIT BEING DISPLAYED BY YOU HAS BROUGHT AMERICA TO ITS FEET AS ONE MAN. YOUR HEROIC SUCCESS AGAINST SUCH EXTREME ODDS AND DISCOURAGE-MENT HAS SET THE PACE THAT WILL CARRY THIS NATION FORWARD TO VICTORY. WE CONTINUE TO DEPEND UPON YOU. KEEP YOUR HEADS HIGH AND YOUR CHINS UP. YOUR COUNTRY WILL NOT FAIL YOU.
—MESSAGE FROM GENERAL HENRY H. ARNOLD TO GENERAL LEWIS
H. BRERETON, 13 DECEMBER 1941

Across from the PX there stood the base theatre which boasted the latest movie thrillers, the latest Walt Disney creation, and a long line of waiting soldiers. The furnishings inside the theatre were not luxurious—they were not even comfortable —but any complaint would bring the reply: "Ain't ya' heard there's a war on?"

—PERSONAL ACCOUNT

Guadalcanal Jim's Barber Shop

Shrapnel Clip; Zero Trim or

The Fox Hole Bob

25 cents

Moose grease—35 cents

—words on a sign in a U.S. Marine

Corps barber shop, 1943

F4U CORSAIR (FOREGROUND)

TBM AVENGERS (FOREGROUND)

January 1944—Japan and Germany lost all the major battles of the year, signaling their weakening war effort and the close of the war, while at home Congress created a five-star general rank and Bing Crosby serenaded the nation with "Going My Way."

F6F HELLCAT

KAMIKAZE ATTACK, U.S.S. BUNKER HILL

TBM AVENGERS

April (1945) brought world-startling news with the death of our commander-in-chief, President Franklin Delano Roosevelt, who died April 12 at the age of 63. This, however, did not stop, or even slow, the war effort, and Russia announced that Berlin was completely encircled....Death struck a second sad blow during April when the invasion of Okinawa brought the headline: Death Comes to GI's Pal, Ernie Pyle.

F6F HELLCATS

When the Teatro Mercantile was not presenting operas or stage shows, GI's would fill its hard wooden seats to watch the latest cinema antics of Bing Crosby, Betty Hutton, Abbott and Costello, or Bette Davis. Directed by the Red Cross and the Army Special Services, most of the more recent movie productions were shown on the screen of the Italian theatre with, of course, a five minute wait every half hour while the operator changed reels. These movies, however, were an escape from the country that we were in, an escape from the life that we were living. Once again we could see America, an automobile, a nightclub, a well-dressed woman. Our over-taxed memories could relax, and we would be walking once more on the sidewalks of Broadway, Main Street, Water Street, Fifth Avenue, or Sunset Boulevard.

—PERSONAL ACCOUNT

B-29 SUPERFORTRESS

B-29 SUPERFORTRESS

Take advantage of opportunities afforded you when the air-raid sirens sound

the warning of attack or blackout.   For example:

    A. If in a bakery, grab a pie.

    B. If in a tavern, grab a beer.

    C. If in a theater, grab a blonde.

—a wag's response to air-raid instructions in Hawaii after the bombing of Pearl Harbor,

December 1941

INVASION FORCE

The tempo of a successful war is progressive. We have to do all we can and then immediately double it. The enemy can stand the kind of blows that we gave him last year even though they were heavy and though they hurt him. What he cannot stand and what we can and must give him are those redoubled blows.

—SPEECH BY GENERAL HENRY H. ARNOLD, 30 DECEMBER 1943

P-47 THUNDERBOLT

P-40 WARHAWK

We have learned how to win a war in
this air age. Our best hope for a long
and secure peace lies in remembering
what we have learned.

—Robert A. Lovett, Assistant Secretary of

War for Air, September 1944

CLASSICS would have been impossible without the help of many friends, businesses, and supporters. To find, fly, and photograph the aircraft you see on these pages took three years of planning and a year and a half of shooting. These color pictures were selected from over 10,000 35mm slides, and present a cross section of the finest restored World War II aircraft in the world. Each of these airplanes is a flying work of art, representing thousands of hours of effort and major amounts of money to restore, fly, and maintain. In a sense, this book is a museum catalog of some of America's finest flying warbirds.

Air-to-air photography is difficult without superb pilots, planning, and precise execution. Robbie Robinson, Dale Krebsbach, and Jack Moore flew the B-25 camera plane for most of the air-to-air photography in CLASSICS. Bill Arnot, Mike Pupich, Craig Timms, and R.L. Waltrip also loaned their B-25s as camera planes when Robbie's B-25, "Chapter XI," was not available. These marvelous airplanes provided a first-class seat facing aft for me to take pictures. I was privileged to work with some of the best warbird pilots flying today. Gentlemen like Howard Pardue, Rudy Frasca, Hess Bomberger, Pete McManus, Archie Donahue, and J.K. West flew formation on my camera ship, sometimes so close that I could read their lips as we talked on the radio. I would have been unable to make these pictures without the skills of these and many other pilots and aircrews who flew for my cameras. Thanks again to all of you.

I must also thank Arnold Drapkin and the editors at TIME magazine for giving me the time and encouragement to tackle the huge project that CLASSICS became. To the photojournalist, time and access are priceless commodities: TIME helped with both. Kodachrome film and Leica cameras faithfully captured the scenes that unfolded, flight after flight. Most of the shooting for CLASSICS was done with Leica R4 cameras, and 35mm, 90mm, and 180mm lenses. The new 35mm 1.4 Summilux became a kind of time machine for me during the hectic days of shooting. With its added ability to gather light, I was able to shoot one-half hour earlier and one-half hour later each day. This bonus of extra time allowed me to capture a very special kind of light and mood which can be seen throughout CLASSICS.

As always, safety was our first concern during the shooting of this book. My friend and assistant, Ted Reynolds, and I wore safety gear from Adventure Specialists in Miami, Florida, for each flight. Many times I was looking out through nothing but air and sunshine to the plane I was photographing. With a dependable safety harness on, I had one less thing to worry about. Ken Hansen and his staff came to my rescue during the shooting of CLASSICS. Being able to replace a broken camera or lens overnight from Ken's stock of Leica equipment was invaluable.

Unintentionally, I'm sure I've left out people who helped make CLASSICS a reality. To each of you who helped change this dream into a book we can hold in our hands, thank you!

— MARK MEYER

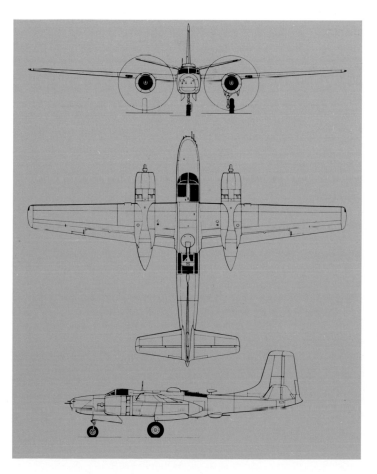

A-26 INVADER

The powerful, quick, and heavily armed A-26 Invader was designed in 1940, and the first prototype flew in July 1942. This aircraft—the culmination of the development of the A-20 series—was one of the best ground-attack and tactical bombers used by the United States.

Heavy machine guns were mounted in the nose section, and four additional heavy machine guns were installed in remote-control turrets. The power of this aircraft lay in its ability to add another ten externally mounted machine guns on certain missions. When this extra strength was coupled with the Invader's formidable bomb-load, the aircraft possessed lethal power.

The A-26C, the last of the three Invader variants, was completed in 1945. It was a more conventionally designed aircraft, having a glazed nose and less armament.

After the end of the war, the A-26 Invader remained in service, and these aircraft played an active part in both the Korean and Vietnam wars.

Manufacturer: Douglas Aircraft Company **Type:** bomber, ground-attack **Engine:** two Pratt & Whitney R-2800-27 Double Wasp 18-cylinder radial air-cooled, 2,000 hp each **Dimensions:** wingspan 70 feet, length 50 feet 9 inches, height 18 feet 6 inches **Weight:** 35,000 pounds (loaded) **Speed:** 355 mph maximum, 280 mph cruise **Ceiling:** 31,300 feet **Range:** 1,800 miles **Armament:** 10 machine guns, 4,000 pounds of bombs **Crew:** 3

Photographs: p. 102

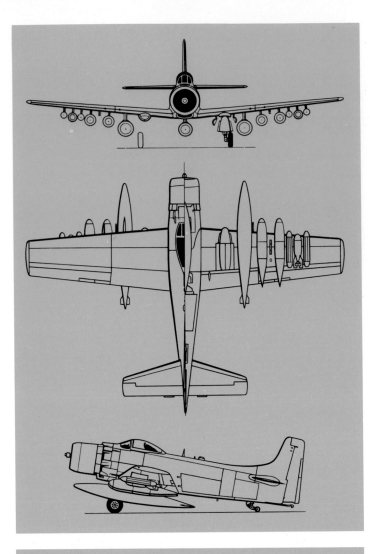

AD-1 SKYRAIDER

Between 1945 and 1957 seven versions of the Skyraider were produced. The first prototype, the XBT2D-1, flew in March 1945, less than one year after the project began. By December 1946, the first AD-1 models flew into combat. The great potential of its airframe led to the development of new variants, which were the last of the heavy, single-seat, piston-engine, combat aircraft developed.

From the beginning, the AD Skyraider series showed great potential, and each model incorporated additional enhancements. One common feature shared by earlier variants was their ability to fly as day-assault, all-weather assault, radar surveillance, or electronic countermeasures air-craft.

The AD-5, designed in 1951, was a sophisticated aircraft with enough space for two crewmen to sit side-by-side in a wide cockpit. This innovative design was discarded in 1952, however, with the production of the single-seat assault configuration of the AD-6 and the powerful AD-7, produced in 1955.

The versatility of the AD Skyraider family kept the aircraft in action through the late 1970s as a ground-attack plane.

Manufacturer: Douglas Aircraft Company **Type:** reconnaissance, ground-attack **Engine:** Wright R-3350-26W Cyclone 18-cylinder radial air-cooled, 2,700 hp **Dimensions:** wingspan 50 feet; length AD-5W—40 feet 1 inch, AD-6—39 feet 2 inches; height AD-5W—15 feet 10 inches, AD-6—15 feet 8 inches **Weight:** 25,500 pounds (loaded) **Speed:** AD-5W—311 mph maximum at 18,000 feet; AD-6—322 mph maximum at 18,000 feet **Ceiling:** AD-5W—27,000 feet; AD-6—28,500 feet **Range:** AD-5W—1,294 miles; AD-6—1,143 miles **Armament:** AD-5W—2 × 20mm cannon; AD-6—4 × 20mm cannon, 8,000 pounds of bombs **Crew:** AD-5W—3; AD-6—1

Photographs: pp. 90-91, p. 92, p.93

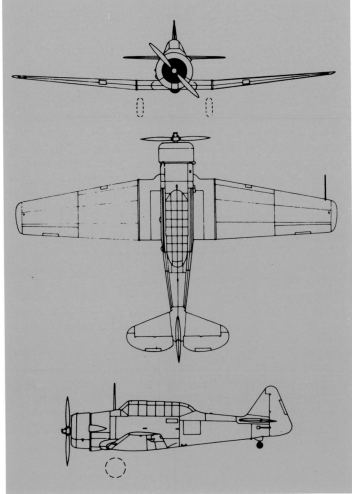

AT-6 TEXAN

The first production models of the AT-6 Texan appeared in the U.S. in 1940 and were the "twin" of the Australian Wirraway, manufactured by Commonwealth Aircraft. Although the new aircraft incorporated many of the latest technological advancements, the AT-6 maintained the same general lines and structure of its predecessor, North American's BT-9 trainer. (Earlier the BT-9 had been improved to create the NA-33, which the Australians had adopted for their Wirraway line.) The main difference between the AT-6 and the BT-9 was the Texan's new, retractable landing-gear.

Five variants of the AT-6 were produced, and small modifications were made to each new model. The AT-6A utilized a different engine and fuel tanks; the AT-6B was intended for use in airgunner training; the AT-6C introduced specific structural modifications to save aluminum; the AT-6D returned to the original design. The final design, the AT-6F, was also the most powerful.

AT-6 Texan monoplanes proved to be so safe and durable that today the planes are still used by many military air forces.

Manufacturer: North American Aviation, Inc. **Type:** trainer **Engine:** AT-6A—Pratt & Whitney R-1340-49 Wasp 9-cylinder radial air-cooled, 600 hp **Dimensions:** wingspan 42 feet, length 29 feet, height 11 feet 9 inches **Weight:** 5,300 pounds (loaded) **Speed:** 208 mph maximum **Ceiling:** 24,200 feet **Range:** 750 miles **Armament:** 2 machine guns **Crew:** 2

Photographs: pp. 48-49; NA-33, p. 52; p. 53

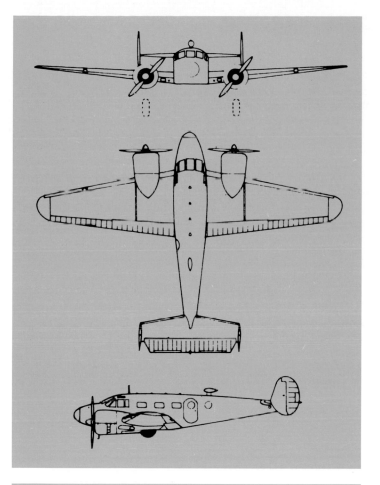

AT-11 KANSAN

The AT-11 trainer was a modified version of the C-45 Expeditor transport. Like most of the best military transport planes in the United States, the Expeditor was based on the designs of a civil aircraft, the Beech C-78.

Of the more than 4,000 C-78s produced, approximately 1,400 of them were C-45s. This light, twin-engine transport sparked the Army's interest in 1941 because of its versatility, and the original order for 11 was increased the following year. The AT-7 and AT-11 training variants and the F2 photo-reconnaissance variants were all produced from the C-45.

Manufacturer: Beech Aircraft Corporation **Type:** trainer **Engine:** two Pratt & Whitney R-985 AN 1 Wasp Junior 9-cylinder radial air-cooled, 450 hp each **Dimensions:** wingspan 47 feet 8 inches, length 34 feet 3 inches, height 9 feet 8 inches **Weight:** 8,727 pounds (loaded) **Speed:** 215 mph maximum **Ceiling:** 20,000 feet **Range:** 700 miles **Armament:** none **Crew:** 2

Photographs: pp. 50-51

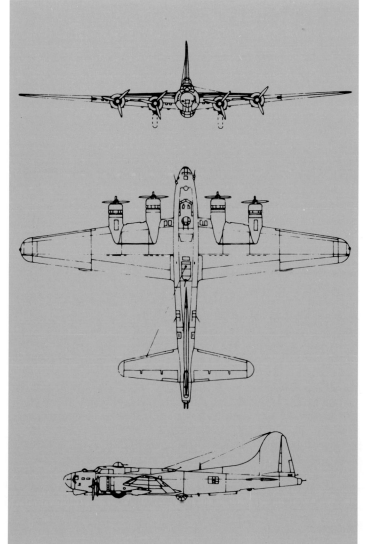

B-17 FLYING FORTRESS

Despite the Army Air Corps' request for a multi-engine (meaning twin-engine), anti-ship bomber, Boeing designed the Model 299 with four of the most powerful engines available. After prolonged tests and evaluations, the B-17B Fortress was fitted with the General Electric turbo-supercharger and delivered in June 1939.

From the beginning, the B-17 was popular because of its conservative wing loading, even though the aircraft's low cruising speed meant that it was unsteady during emergency escapes when both pilots had left their seats.

By 1942 the B-17C, D, and E had all been produced with various improvements. The B-17F, flown in April of that year, was fitted with a plexiglass nose and paddle-blade propellers, along with more than 400 other minor improvements. The final production model, the G, had a chin turret to discourage head-on attacks.

After manufacture of the Fortress stopped in April 1945, some were converted into YB-40 escort fighters or BQ-7 radio-controlled missiles. Still others served as tankers, strategic reconnaissance aircraft, transports, and air/sea rescue lifeboat carriers.

Manufacturer: Boeing Aircraft Company **Type:** bomber **Engine:** four Wright Cyclone 9-cylinder radial air-cooled, 1,200 hp each; B-17E—R-1820-65; B-17F/G—R-1820-97 **Dimensions:** wingspan 103 feet 9 inches; length B-17C—67 feet 11 inches, B-17E—73 feet 10 inches, B-17F/G—74 feet 9 inches; height B-17E—19 feet 2 inches, B-17F/G—19 feet 1 inch **Weight:** B-17C—49,650 pounds (loaded); B-17E—53,000 pounds (loaded); B-17G—65,500 pounds (loaded) **Speed:** B-17C—323 mph maximum; B-17E—317 mph maximum at 25,000 feet; B-17F—299 mph maximum at 25,000 feet, 162 mph cruise; B-17G—287 mph maximum at 25,000 feet **Ceiling:** B-17C—37,000 feet; B-17E—36,000 feet; B-17F—35,000 feet (service); B-17G—35,600 feet **Range:** B-17E—3,000 miles; B-17F—3,600 miles (maximum), 2,100 with 4,000 pounds (combat); B-17G—3,400 miles **Armament:** 17,600 pounds of bombs; B-17E—10-13 machine guns; B-17F/G—13 machine guns **Crew:** B-17E—9, B-17G—10

Photographs: pp. 2-3, pp. 8-9, pp. 22-23, p. 24, p. 25, p. 26, pp. 28-29, p. 33

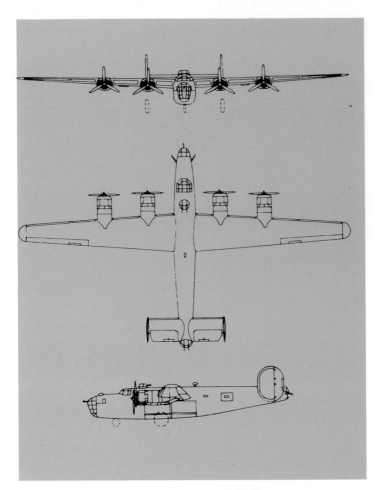

B-24 LIBERATOR

B-24s were used by Allied air forces on every front of the war in capacities ranging from naval reconnaissance to submarine warfare to transport. The original prototype, Model 32, flew in December 1939, and over the next 18 months, turbocharged engines, armor, self-sealing tanks, and defensive armament were added to improve the quality of the aircraft.

Fundamental features of the Liberator included the long, aerodynamically efficient Davis wing, tall main landing-gears with single wheels and legs that retracted outward to lie inside the wing, and a stumpy fuselage.

The B-24D began to emerge by the end of 1941, proving to be a good performer at high altitudes. There were few changes until the B-24G, which introduced a nose turret, and later the 24L, which used a lightweight, twin-gun tail position instead of a powered turret, and finally the 24N version, the first to use a single fin.

Manufacturer: Consolidated Aircraft Corporation **Type:** bomber **Engine:** four Pratt & Whitney Twin Wasp 14-cylinder radial air-cooled, 1,200 hp each; B-24D—R-1830-43; B-24H/J—R-1830-65 **Dimensions:** wingspan B-24D/H—110 feet, B-24J—67 feet 2 inches; length B-24D—66 feet 4 inches, B-24H/J—67 feet 2 inches; height B-24D—17 feet 11 inches, B-24H/J—18 feet **Weight:** B-24D—60,000 pounds (loaded); B-24J—65,000 pounds (loaded) **Speed:** B-24D—303 mph maximum at 25,000 feet; B-24H—313 mph maximum at 25,000 feet, 215 mph cruise; B-24J—300 mph at 25,000 feet **Ceiling:** B-24D—32,000 feet; B-24H/J—28,000 feet **Range:** B-24D—2,850 miles; B-24H—3,700 miles (maximum), 2,100 miles (combat); B-24J—2,100 miles **Armament:** 10 machine guns; B-24B—8,000 pounds of bombs; B-24H—12,800 pounds of bombs (maximum), 5,000 pounds of bombs (combat) **Crew:** B-24D—8-10; B-24J—8-12

Photographs: pp. 34-35, p.36

B-25 MITCHELL

The first prototype of the B-25 Mitchell, the NA-40, was built in 1939. Designed with Twin Wasp engines, the NA-40 underwent changes almost immediately to meet revised Army specifications. The NA-62 replacement model employed a more powerful engine. It was followed in 1940 by the B-25, which was supplied to almost every Allied air force during the war.

Several versions of the Mitchell were introduced between 1943 and 1944. Recognizing that heavy nose armament was needed for low-level attacks in the Pacific, especially on ships, North American modified 175 B-25Bs in the field with ten 0.5-inch (12.7mm) guns that fired ahead.

Additional changes were also made to the B-25H and the B-25J. The H model was the first revised with rear armament and a dorsal turret just behind the cockpit; the J was outfitted with either a glazed nose for a navigator/bombardier or a solid nose containing a battery of heavy machine guns.

Manufacturer: North American Aviation, Inc. **Type:** bomber **Engine:** two Wright Cyclone 14-cylinder radial air-cooled, 1,700 hp each; B-25A—R-2600-9; B-25H—R-2600-13; B-25J—R-2600-92 **Dimensions:** wingspan 67 feet 7 inches; length B-25A—54 feet 1 inch, B-25B/C/J—52 feet 11 inches, B-25G/H—51 feet; height B-25A—15 feet 10 inches, B-25G/H—15 feet 9 inches, B-25J—16 feet 4 inches **Weight:** B-25A—27,000 pounds (loaded); B-25C—34,000 pounds (loaded); B-25H—36,047 pounds (loaded); B-25J—35,000 pounds (loaded) **Speed:** B-25A—315 mph maximum at 15,000 feet; B-25B—300 mph maximum; B-25G—281 mph maximum at 15,000 feet, 200 mph cruise; B-25H—275 mph maximum at 13,000 feet; B-25J—272 mph maximum at 13,000 feet **Ceiling:** B-25A—27,000 feet; B-25G—25,000 feet (service); B-25H—23,800 feet; B-25J—24,200 feet **Range:** B-25A/H/J—1,350 miles; B-25G—2,400 miles (maximum), 1,560 miles with 3,000 pounds (combat) **Armament:** B-25A—5 machine guns, 3,000 pounds of bombs; B-25G—1 × 75mm cannon, 18 machine guns, 3,000 pounds of bombs; B-25H—1 × 75mm cannon, 14 machine guns, 3,200 pounds of bombs **Crew:** 5

Photographs: p. 4, p. 103, pp. 104-105, p. 106, p. 107, p. 109, pp. 110-111, p. 111, pp. 112-113

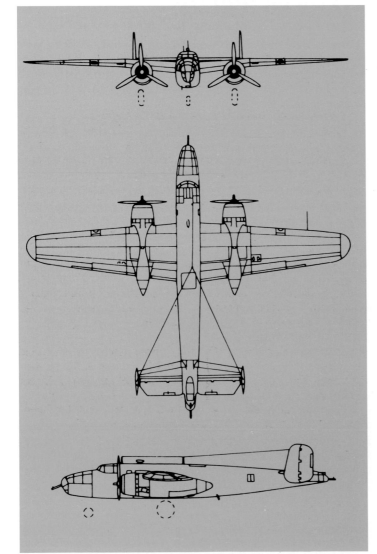

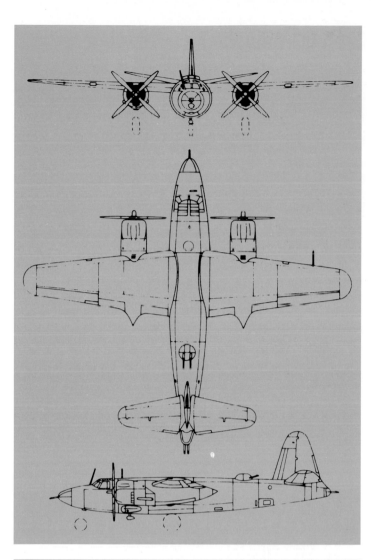

B-26 MARAUDER

The B-26 Marauder was built in response to specifications for a medium bomber that could successfully achieve requested speed, range, and operational altitude. The design plan, submitted within six months of the January 1939 request, appeared to fulfill all requirements, and an order for 1,000 was placed without the development of a prototype—an unprecedented action.

The first B-26 was delivered in 1941, and at that time, the aircraft's weakness was noticed. Due to the high wing-loading feature, the plane required high and dangerous landing speeds. This greatly disturbed pilots and crew, badly shaking their confidence, and making proper training difficult.

At one point a commission was appointed to study the situation, stopping production until after the inquiry. Their decision was to continue production of the B-26, but with an amended design to make the aircraft easier to handle.

Despite this problem, the twin-engine Marauder saw action on all fronts between 1942 and 1945.

Manufacturer: Glenn L. Martin Company **Type:** bomber **Engine:** two Pratt & Whitney Double Wasp 18-cylinder radial air-cooled, 2,000 hp each; B-26B—R-2800-41; B-26G—R-2800-43 **Dimensions:** wingspan B-26B 65 feet, B-26G—71 feet; length B-26B—58 feet 3 inches, B-26G—56 feet 1 inch; height B-26B—19 feet 10 inches, B-26G—20 feet 4 inches **Weight:** B-26B—34,000 pounds (loaded); B-26G—38,200 pounds (loaded) **Speed:** B-26B—317 mph maximum at 14,500 feet; B-26G—283 mph maximum at 5,000 feet, 225 mph cruise **Ceiling:** B-26B—23,500 feet; B-26G—19,800 feet **Range:** B-26B—1,150 miles; B-26G—1,100 miles **Armament:** B-26B—6 machine guns, 3,000 pounds of bombs; B-26G—11 machine guns, 4,000 pounds of bombs **Crew:** 7

Photographs: pp. 114-115, pp. 116-117

B-29 SUPERFORTRESS

In March 1938, Chief of Staff Oscar Westover requested proposals for a strategic bomber that would out-perform the B-17. Boeing answered the challenge, and in January 1939 a nationwide production program began.

Engineering efforts produced the Model 345 design in the summer of 1940, and the first prototype flew without armament in September 1942. From stem to stern, the B-29 used new and revolutionary structure, materials, systems, propulsion, armament, and flight environment. It boasted a pressurized crew compartment in the nose, a tunnel to a second pressurized cabin in the rear fuselage, an all-glazed nose with instrument panels on each side for the two pilots, five powered turrets driven by gunners who could transfer control from one man to another, and vast front and rear bomb bays from which weapons were sequenced to maintain center of gravity.

By 1945 hundreds of crews were manning the B-29, in the opinion of many, the best strategic bomber of World War II. It was the Superfortress that brought an end to the conflict in August 1945.

Manufacturer: Boeing Aircraft Company **Type:** bomber **Engine:** four Wright R-3350-57 Cyclone 18-cylinder radial air-cooled, 2,200 hp each **Dimensions:** wingspan 141 feet 3 inches, length 99 feet, height 29 feet 7 inches **Weight:** 141,000 pounds (loaded) **Speed:** 358 mph maximum at 25,000 feet **Ceiling:** 31,850 feet **Range:** 4,100 miles **Armament:** 1 × 20mm cannon, 10 machine guns, 20,000 pounds of bombs **Crew:** 10

Photographs: p. 14, pp. 118-119

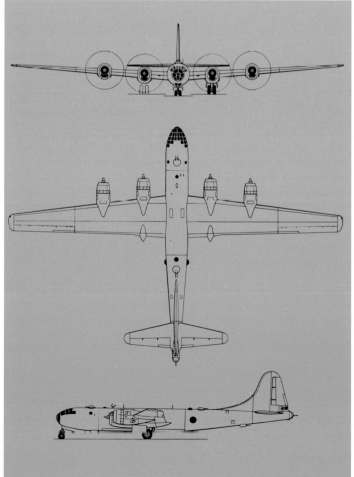

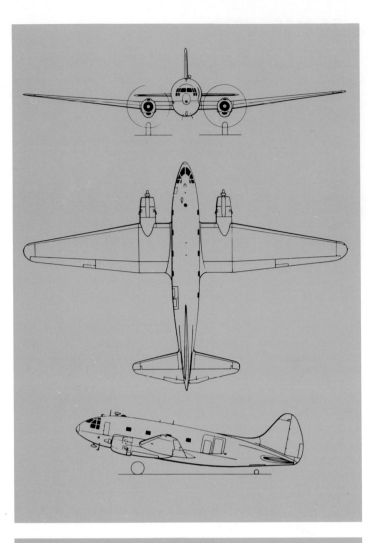

C-46 COMMANDO

Developed to replace the DC-3 in 1937, the C-46 Commando was originally designed as a commercial aircraft. The Army, however, showed immediate interest when the prototype was flown on March 26, 1940, displaying excellent performance capabilities at high altitudes with a high load capacity.

After camouflage and military markings were added, the Commando boosted the transport strength of the U.S. air forces during the second half of WWII. Curtiss built six variants of the transport, all of which saw action mainly in the Pacific. Deliveries of the C-46A began in July 1942, and in 1944 the C-46D, with modified fuselage, was introduced. The C-46E was designed with only one door in the fuselage, while the C-46F employed more powerful engines. A C-46G version tested even more powerful engines, but only one of this model was ever produced.

Manufacturer: Curtiss-Wright Corporation **Type:** transport **Engine:** C-46A— two Pratt & Whitney R-2800-51 Double Wasp 18-cylinder radial air-cooled, 2,000 hp each **Dimensions:** wingspan 108 feet 1 inch, length 76 feet 4 inches, height 21 feet 9 inches **Weight:** 56,000 pounds (loaded) **Speed:** 269 mph maximum at 15,000 feet, 160 mph cruise **Ceiling:** 27,600 feet **Range:** 1,200 miles **Armament:** none **Crew:** 4

Photographs: p. 54

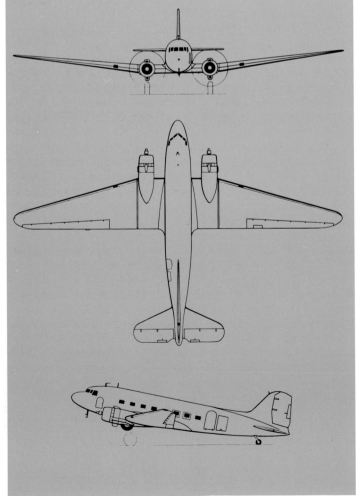

C-47 SKYTRAIN

The C-47 Skytrain was the basic military model of the DC-3. Many versions of the DC-3 were designed and produced, but it was the C-47 Skytrain, with its large side doors, strong freight door, glider tow-attachment, and wooden seats that folded along the sides of the cabin, that made it one of the workhorses of WWII.

All variants were designed with a fatigue-resistant structure, entirely of stressed skin, and with a multi-spar wing that offered a number of alternative load-paths. Advances in flaps, landing gear, propellers, radial cowlings, de-icer boots on the leading edges, and warm and soundproof interiors were incorporated into all versions. Although this meant that the aircraft was heavier, the powerful engines allowed safe flying on one engine, something of which previous transport aircraft were not capable.

The backbone of most of the world's post-war air forces were transports based on the wartime C-47, but by 1980, the use of C-47 variants was restricted to a handful of special test aircraft. Ordinary transport versions, however, were still in service with at least 75 of the world's air forces or paramilitary organizations.

Manufacturer: Douglas Aircraft Company **Type:** transport **Engine:** two Pratt & Whitney R-1830 radial air-cooled, 1,200 hp each **Dimensions:** wingspan 95 feet, length 64 feet 5.5 inches, height 16 feet 11 inches **Weight:** 26,000 pounds (loaded) **Speed:** 230 mph maximum at 9,000 feet, 155 mph cruise **Ceiling:** 29,000 feet (service) **Range:** 2,125 miles (maximum), 1,350 miles (combat) **Armament:** none **Crew:** 4-5

Photographs: p. 57

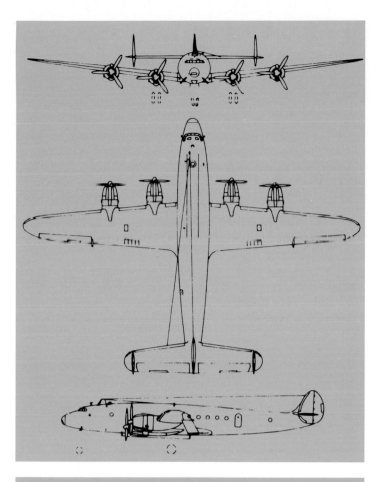

C-69 CONSTELLATION

Late in World War II, the transport arm of the U.S. Army Air Force was strengthened by the Lockheed C-69 Constellation. Originally intended for commercial use, 22 C-69s were in service with the USAAF before the war ended.

The C-69 resulted from a 1939 Trans World Airlines request for a new aircraft. Its prototype, the L-049, first flew on January 9, 1943, and by 1944 the first military version had gone into service.

Manufacturer: Lockheed Aircraft Corporation **Type:** transport **Engine:** four Wright R-3350-35 Cyclone 18-cylinder radial air-cooled, 2,200 hp each **Dimensions:** wingspan 123 feet, length 95 feet 2 inches, height 23 feet 8 inches **Weight:** 72,000 pounds (loaded) **Speed:** 330 mph maximum **Ceiling:** 25,000 feet **Range:** 2,400 miles **Armament:** none **Crew:** 4-5

Photographs: p. 58, p. 59

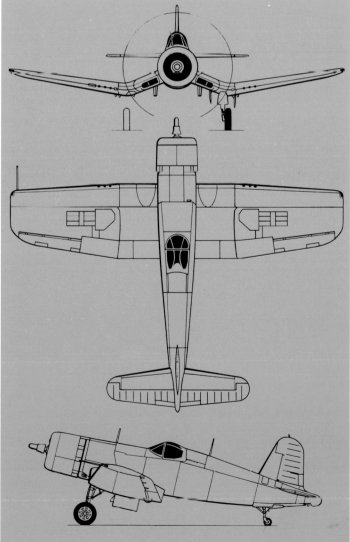

F4U CORSAIR

The prototype of the F4U Corsair had the biggest and most powerful engine, the largest propeller, and probably the largest wing of any fighter in history.

In 1940 after almost being destroyed in a forced landing, the aircraft was rebuilt. A new model, which used an air-cooled engine, was the first fighter, and the first American aircraft of any kind, to exceed 400 mph. Many Navy requirements were incorporated into the V-166 prototype that was first flown in May 1940, including internal cells in the wing for small bombs and a fixed-gun armament comprising two 0.303-inch (7.7mm) Brownings above the engine and two of 0.5-inch (12.7mm) caliber in the wings.

During 1941 the Corsair was redesigned. Despite an increase in weight, the F4U's overall performance was enhanced. Production started up again in late 1941, and over 9,440 F4U-1 aircraft were built, including the 1C and the 1D, which employed different armament or engine models. Corsairs were manufactured until December 1952, one of the longest runs of any piston-engine American fighter.

Manufacturer: Chance Vought Aircraft Division of United Aircraft Corporation **Type:** fighter **Engine:** Pratt & Whitney Double Wasp 18-cylinder radial air-cooled; F4U-1—R-2800-8, 2,000 hp; F4U-1D—R-2800-8W, 2,000 hp; F4U-4—R-2800-18W, 2,100 hp; F4U-5N—R-2800-32W, 2,300 hp **Dimensions:** wingspan 41 feet; length F4U-1/1D—33 feet 4.5 inches, F4U-4—33 feet 8 inches, F4U-5N—34 feet 6 inches; height F4U-1/1D—15 feet 1 inch, F4U-5N—14 feet 9 inches **Weight:** F4U-1—13,120 pounds (loaded); F4U-1D—14,000 pounds (loaded); F4U-4—14,670 pounds (loaded); F4U-5N—14,106 pounds (loaded) **Speed:** F4U-1—417 mph maximum at 19,900 feet; F4U-1D—425 mph maximum at 20,000 feet; F4U-4—466 mph maximum at 26,200 feet; F4U-5N—470 mph maximum **Ceiling:** F4U-1—36,900 feet; F4U-1D—37,000 feet; F4U-4—41,500 feet; F4U-5N—41,600 feet **Range:** F4U-1/1D—1,015 miles; F4U-5N—1,120 miles **Armament:** F4U-1—6 machine guns; F4U-1D—6 machine guns, 2,000 pounds of bombs **Crew:** 1

Photographs: pp. 12-13, pp. 120-121, p. 122, p. 123, p. 125, pp. 126-127, pp. 128-129, p. 130, p. 131, pp. 132-133

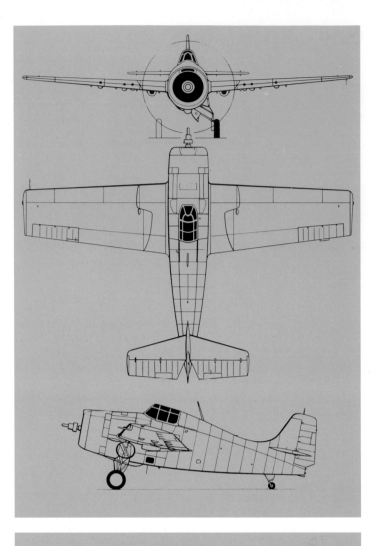

F4F WILDCAT

The U.S. Navy's move from the biplane to the monoplane occurred in 1940, when Grumman Aircraft Engineering Corporation delivered the F4F-3 Wildcat fighter.

After development of the XF4F-2 prototype in September 1937, and the modified XF4F-3 in February 1939, Grumman's F4F fighter became the most important Allied naval fighter during the first half of WWII.

Most versions of the F4F Wildcat had 1,200 hp Twin Wasp engines, a rotund but finely streamlined fuselage, a rectangular mid-wing, skewed hinges to fold the wings alongside the fuselage with upper surface outwards, and typical Grumman landing gears retracting upwards into the fuselage. The F4F was an effective fighter, fast and maneuverable.

Manufacturer: Grumman Aircraft Engineering Corporation **Type:** fighter **Engine:** Pratt & Whitney Twin Wasp 14-cylinder radial air-cooled, 1,200 hp; F4F-3—R-1830-76; F4F-4—R-1830-86 **Dimensions:** wingspan 38 feet, length 28 feet 9 inches, height 11 feet 10 inches **Weight:** F4F-3—7,000 pounds (loaded); F4F-4—7,952 pounds (loaded) **Speed:** F4F-3—331 mph maximum at 21,300 feet; F4F-4—318 mph maximum at 19,400 feet **Ceiling:** F4F-3—37,500 feet; F4F-4—34,900 feet **Range:** F4F-3—845 miles; F4F-4—770 miles **Armament:** F4F-4—6 machine guns, 200 pounds of bombs **Crew:** 1

Photographs: pp. 142-143, p. 148, p. 149

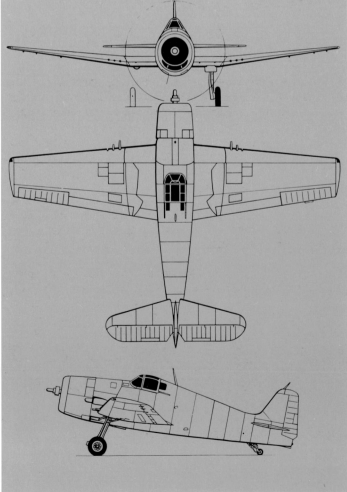

F6F HELLCAT

The F6F Hellcat was a bigger and more powerful naval fighter than its predecessor, the F4F. Responding to the Navy's need for more power after the destruction at Pearl Harbor, the first fighter planes were flown in June 1942 with R-2600 engines.

Almost immediately the XF6F-1 was re-engined, and the successor, the XF6F-3, was designed with the power plant that became standard, the Pratt & Whitney R-2800 Double Wasp. The first of these aircraft flew in October 1942, and deliveries began within 18 months.

The only other significant Hellcat model was the F6F-5, which flew on April 4, 1944. This aircraft had improved cowling and armament capacity. The other variants that Grumman produced incorporated only small modifications, demonstrating the impressive design of the original Hellcat.

Throughout the war the F6F proved to be both tough and maneuverable. When production of the Hellcat series ended in November 1945, more than 12,000 had been produced—this in a three-year period.

Manufacturer: Grumman Aircraft Engineering Corporation **Type:** fighter **Engine:** Pratt & Whitney Double Wasp 18-cylinder radial air-cooled, 2,000 hp; F6F-3(early)—R-2800-10; F6F-3(late)/5—R-2800-10W **Dimensions:** wingspan 42 feet 10 inches, length 33 feet 7 inches, height 13 feet 1 inch **Weight:** F6F-3—11,381 pounds (loaded); F6F-5—15,400 pounds (loaded) **Speed:** F6F-3—376 mph maximum at 17,300 feet; F6F-5—380 mph maximum at 23,400 feet **Ceiling:** F6F-3—38,400 feet; F6F-5—37,300 feet **Range:** F6F-3—1,090 miles; F6F-5—1,040 miles **Armament:** F6F-3—6 machine guns; F6F-5—6 machine guns, 2,000 pounds of bombs **Crew:** 1

Photographs: pp. 142-143, p. 144

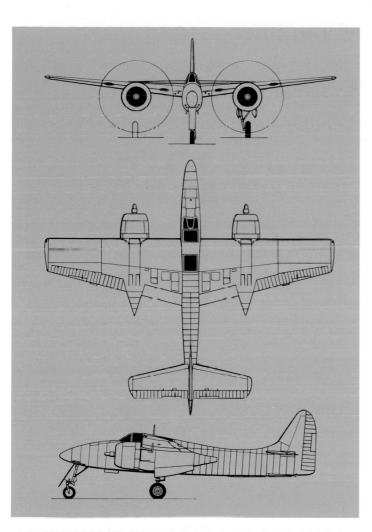

F7F TIGERCAT

In 1941 Grumman Aircraft began designing the F7F Tigercat, which was a conventional, heavy, multirole fighter. The first prototype, designed for the U.S. Navy, was completed in December 1943.

The aircraft displayed exceptional speed, power, and maneuverability. Its twin-engine design, which broke from Grumman tradition, included medium wings and a tricycle undercarriage and was the first of its kind to see carrier-borne service with the Navy.

To correct operational problems in the first version of the Tigercat, the F7F-1, specifications had to be modified. In 1945 the F7F-2N model followed. This was a two-seat night fighter. The war was brought to a close before the F7F-3, a single-seat plane, could see action.

Production continued after the end of WWII. In 1946 the assembly lines produced F7F-3Ns and F7F-4s, both night fighters. Used by the U.S. Marine Corps, the Tigercat saw action until the first stages of the Korean War.

Manufacturer: Grumman Aircraft Engineering Corporation **Type:** night fighter **Engine:** F7F-3N—two Pratt & Whitney R-2800-34W Double Wasp 18-cylinder radial air-cooled, 2,100 hp each **Dimensions:** wingspan 51 feet 6 inches, length 46 feet 10 inches, height 16 feet 7 inches **Weight:** 25,720 pounds (loaded) **Speed:** 435 mph maximum at 22,200 feet **Ceiling:** 40,700 feet **Range:** 1,200 miles **Armament:** 4 × 20mm cannon **Crew:** 2

Photographs: pp. 142-143, p. 150, p. 151, pp. 152-153, p. 154, p. 155

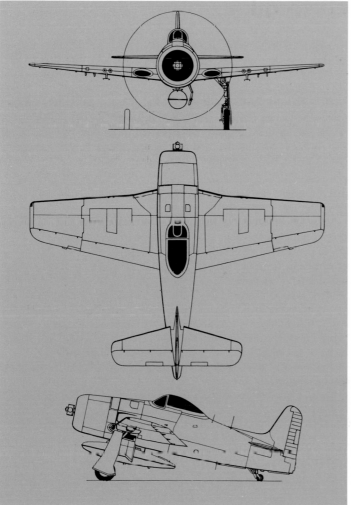

F8F BEARCAT

In 1943 the F8F Bearcat was designed to replace the F6F Hellcat, and in August 1944, the first of the F8F family flew. Two months later, a U.S. Navy order was placed, and production began.

These night fighters were used as part of a wide-ranging program of modernization which took place while the Navy waited for the first jet planes to come into service. During the final stages of the war, over 800 Bearcats were delivered to squadrons.

The F8F, a single-seat, single-engine shipboard interceptor and fighter-bomber, was used by Allied forces after the end of the war. From 1948 to 1950, the F8F-1D was supplied to France, and in 1954, the F8F-1 was supplied to the Thai Air Force.

The Bearcat is considered to be one of the best single-seat, carrier-borne, piston-engine aircraft ever produced. It was introduced too late in WWII to see combat, but the airplane had exceptional performance, and for a time, held the world record for the fastest climb to 10,000 feet.

Manufacturer: Grumman Aircraft Engineering Corporation **Type:** fighter **Engine:** F8F-1B—Pratt & Whitney R-2800-34W Double Wasp 18-cylinder radial air-cooled, 2,100 hp **Dimensions:** wingspan F8F-1B—35 feet 10 inches, F8F-2—35 feet 6 inches; length F8F-1B—28 feet 3 inches, F8F-2—27 feet 8 inches; height F8F-1B—13 feet 10 inches, F8F-2—12 feet 2 inches **Weight:** F8F-1B—12,947 pounds (loaded); F8F-2—13,494 pounds (loaded) **Speed:** F8F-1B—421 mph maximum at 19,700 feet; F8F-2—447 mph maximum **Ceiling:** F8F-1B—38,700 feet; F8F-2—40,700 feet **Range:** F8F-1B—1,105 miles; F8F-2—1,435 miles **Armament:** 4 × 20mm cannon **Crew:** 1

Photographs: pp. 142-143, p. 145, pp. 146-147, p. 147

F9F PANTHER

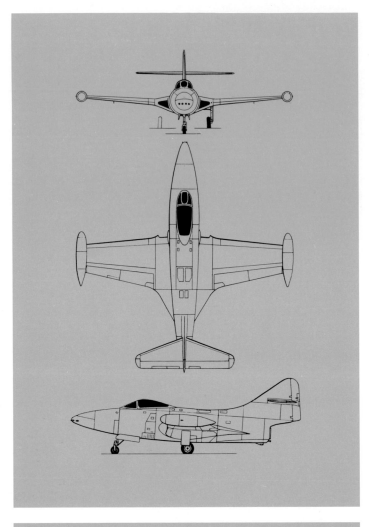

Although the first U.S. Navy jet planes saw action in Korea in 1950, they were the direct result of Grumman Aircraft's response to a Navy request for development of a night fighter during WWII.

The design for Grumman's F9F Panther-Cougar series was initiated during the final stages of the war, and the effort represented the company's first attempt to produce a jet aircraft. Problems beset the project from the beginning, and progress was slow.

It wasn't until November 1947 that the first prototype flew. The development had encountered so many delays that at the time of the test flight, specifications had changed, and the Navy was now interested in purchasing a day fighter.

The F9F-2 variant was chosen for production, and two other models followed, each with a more powerful engine.

Grumman continued to work on the F9F series, incorporating the latest equipment and adding more powerful engines. In 1951, the F6F was introduced, and the Panther was renamed Cougar. The series remained in service until the late 1970s.

Manufacturer: Grumman Aircraft Engineering Corporation **Type:** fighter **Engine:** F9F-2—Pratt & Whitney J42-P-6 turbojet, 5,000 pounds thrust **Dimensions:** wingspan 38 feet, length 37 feet 3 inches, height 11 feet 4 inches **Weight:** 19,452 pounds (loaded) **Speed:** 526 mph maximum at 22,200 feet **Ceiling:** 44,600 feet **Range:** 1,353 miles **Armament:** 4×20mm cannon, 2,000 pounds of bombs **Crew:** 1

Photographs: pp. 156-157, p. 158, p. 159

P2V NEPTUNE

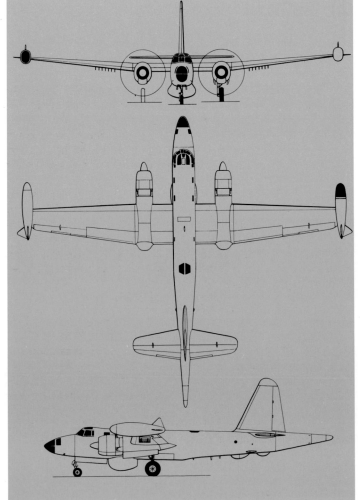

From the end of WWII until the beginning of the 1960s, the Lockheed P2V Neptune was the standard maritime reconnaissance and antisubmarine warfare aircraft of the U.S. Navy. The twin, piston-engine plane was first designed in April 1944, and the prototype flew on May 17, 1945.

It wasn't until the P2V-5 model that twin turbo-jets were employed, in addition to the two piston-engines, to improve the aircraft's performance. This design remained in use until production of the Neptune was halted.

On April 26, 1954, the Neptune reached its final development stage with the introduction of the P2V-7 prototype.

The P2V Neptune was an all-weather, long-range, land-based, antisubmarine aircraft. Its successful design made it an essential part of patrol squadrons from 1947 to 1962.

For ten years, the P2V Neptune was manufactured, and in that time seven different models were produced for use in 11 countries.

Manufacturer: Lockheed Aircraft Corporation **Type:** reconnaissance/antisubmarine **Engine:** P2V-7—two Wright R-3350-32-W Cyclone 18-cylinder radial air-cooled, 3,500 hp each, and two Westinghouse J34-WE-34 turbojets, 3,400 pounds thrust each **Dimensions:** wingspan 103 feet 10 inches, length 91 feet 4 inches, height 29 feet 4 inches **Weight:** 75,500 pounds (loaded) **Speed:** 345 mph maximum at 10,000 feet **Ceiling:** 22,000 feet **Range:** 2,200 miles **Armament:** none **Crew:** 9-10

Photographs: pp. 60-61

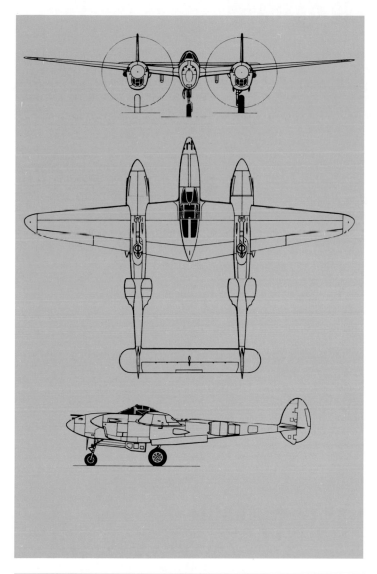

P-38 LIGHTNING

In 1937 the Army wanted an aircraft that would travel at 360 mph at medium altitude, endure at that speed for one hour, and reach optimum altitude in six minutes. The Lockheed 22 was the answer. With two newly developed Allison engines, ducts leading to and from turbochargers in the tops of long tail booms, pipes linking the engines to coolant radiators on the sides of the booms, and a battery of guns in the nose of a small central nacelle, the aircraft was a radical concept.

The first prototype, XP-38, flew in January 1939, and it broke all U.S. transcontinental records. In August 1941 the P-38D was produced, incorporating a laminar-flow wing, Fowler flaps, intercoolers in the leading edges, a pull-out step at the rear of the nacelle for climbing aboard, and an aileron control wheel in the cockpit. It was probably the quietest fighter in history.

Over the years many Lightning variants were produced that featured changes such as inner wings for tanks or bombs, additional power, a new radio, increased external bomb-load, hydraulically boosted ailerons, small powered dive-flaps under the center section, and underwing attachments for rockets.

Manufacturer: Lockheed Aircraft Corporation **Type:** fighter **Engine:** two Allison 12-cylinder V liquid-cooled; P-38F—V-1710-49, 1,250 hp each; P-38H/G/J—V-1710-91, 1,425 hp each; P-38L—V-1710-111, 1,600 hp each **Dimensions:** wingspan 52 feet, length 37 feet 10 inches, height 9 feet 10 inches **Weight:** P-38F—20,000 pounds (loaded); P38J—21,600 pounds (loaded) **Speed:** P-38F—395 mph maximum at 25,000 feet; P-38G—400 mph maximum; P-38H—402 mph maximum at 25,000 feet, 300 mph cruise; P-38J/L—414 mph maximum at 25,000 feet **Ceiling:** P-38F—39,000 feet; P-38H/J/L—44,000 feet **Range:** P-38F/G—1,425 miles; P-38H—2,400 miles with external tanks, 350 miles (combat); P-38J/L—2,260 miles **Armament:** 1 × 20mm cannon, 4 machine guns; P-38F—2,000 pounds of bombs; P-38H—4,000 pounds of bombs; P-38J—3,200 pounds of bombs **Crew:** 1

Photographs: pp. 62-63, p. 64, p. 65, pp. 68-69, p. 70, p. 71, pp. 72-73

P-39 AIRACOBRA

The Bell Aircraft P-39 made its first flight in April 1939. It had several unique features, including a 37mm cannon installed in the nose which fired through the hub of the propeller. As a result, the engine was placed behind the cockpit to maintain the center of gravity and to achieve maximum maneuverability. The long propeller shaft passed between the pilot's legs. Facilitating the installation of heavy gun armament in the nose, the configuration also protected the pilot from behind.

The Airacobra prototype demonstrated excellent, all-round performance. A turbo-supercharged engine drove the aircraft at 390 mph at medium altitudes, probably faster than any other fighter at that time.

Later the supercharged engine was replaced with an unsupercharged one, resulting in a serious lack of power at high altitudes. The extra weight added by the installation of armament and armor plating further decreased the aircraft's performance.

Production of the Airacobra stopped in July 1944.

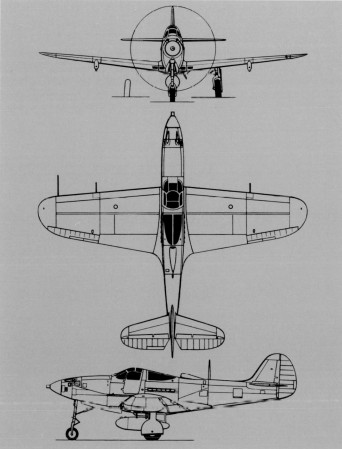

Manufacturer: Bell Aircraft Corporation **Type:** fighter **Engine:** Allison 12-cylinder V liquid-cooled; P-39C/D/F—V-1710-35, 1,150 hp; P-39K/L—V-1710-63, 1,325 hp; P-39M/N/Q—V-1710-85, 1,200 hp **Dimensions:** wingspan 34 feet; length 30 feet 2 inches; height P-39D—11 feet 10 inches, P-39Q—12 feet 5 inches **Weight:** P-39D—7,845 pounds (loaded); P-39L—7,780 pounds (loaded); P-39Q—8,300 pounds (loaded) **Speed:** P-39D—335 mph maximum at 13,800 feet; P-39Q—385 mph maximum at 11,000 feet, 213 mph cruise **Ceiling:** P-39D—29,000 feet; P-39Q—35,000 feet **Range:** P-39D—600 miles; P-39Q—750 miles with 500 pounds of bombs, 1,595 miles (ferry) **Armament:** 1 × 37mm cannon, 4 machine guns, 500 pounds of bombs **Crew:** 1

Photographs: p. 74, p. 75

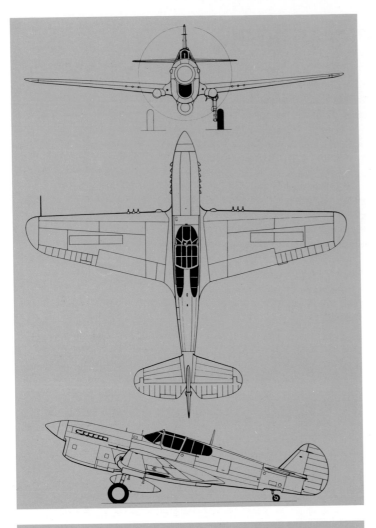

P-40 WARHAWK

Model 75, Curtiss Aircraft's first prototype of the P-40 Warhawk, flew in May 1935, was replaced by the P-36 in March 1937, and resulted in the P-40 in May 1940. Curtiss Aircraft's first stressed-skin, monoplane fighter, designed with wheels that retracted backwards into the wings, the Warhawk was the most important American fighter during the first two years of WWII.

Improved versions of the P-40 were produced, but the overall performance and maneuverability of the aircraft were a constant problem. The Warhawk did have one advantage. After sustaining severe damage during battle, the aircraft was unusually successful in flying safely back to base. This capability played an important part in the controversial decision to continue production of P-40 Warhawks until December 1944, long after superior fighters had been introduced into the U.S. inventory.

Manufacturer: Curtiss-Wright Corporation **Type:** fighter **Engine:** 12-cylinder V liquid-cooled; P-40B/C—Allison V-1710-33, 1,040 hp; P-40K—Allison V-1710-73, 1,325 hp; P-40N—Allison V-1710-81, 1,360 hp **Dimensions:** wingspan 37 feet 4 inches; length P-40B—31 feet 9 inches, P-40E—31 feet 2 inches, P-40C/F/K/N—33 feet 4 inches; height P-40B/E—10 feet 7 inches, P-40F/N—10 feet 4 inches, P-40K—12 feet 5 inches **Weight:** P-40B—7,600 pounds; P-40E—9,200 pounds; P-40F—9,350 pounds; P-40N—8,850 pounds **Speed:** P-40B—352 mph maximum at 15,000 feet; P-40E—354 mph maximum at 15,000 feet; P-40F—364 mph maximum at 20,000 feet; P-40K—362 mph maximum at 15,000 feet; P-40N—378 mph maximum at 10,500 feet, 290 mph cruise **Ceiling:** P-40B—32,400 feet; P-40E—29,000 feet; P-40F—34,400 feet; P-40N—38,000 feet **Range:** P-40B—940 miles; P-40E—850 miles; P-40F—375 miles; P-40K—1,600 miles or 350 miles with 500 pounds; P-40N—240 miles **Armament:** P-40B—4 machine guns; P-40E—6 machine guns, 700 pounds of bombs; P-40F/N—6 machine guns, 500 pounds of bombs; **Crew:** 1

Photographs: pp. 10-11, pp. 94-95, p. 96, p. 97, pp. 100-101

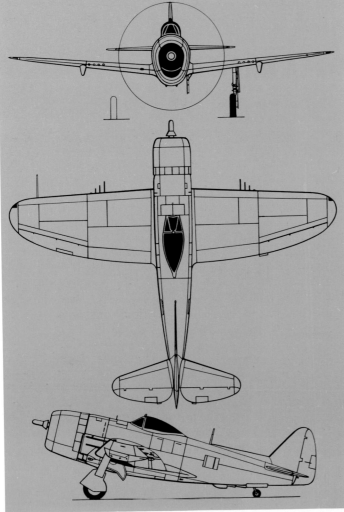

P-47 THUNDERBOLT

In 1933 the first P-47 Thunderbolt design was completed. After undergoing several changes, the P-47 was modified in 1939 in response to combat reports from Europe that indicated a need for more guns and more horsepower.

The first of these new fighters flew in May 1941, and by March 1942, production P-47s were in the air. In early 1943 the 47D model introduced many new features—a refined engine, turbo, and intercooler installation; more armor; increased ammunition and weapon loads; a completely transparent bubble canopy; a universal wing capable of carrying tanks, bombs or rockets; a stronger belly attachment for heavier tanks and bombs; and broad paddle-blade propellers.

Excelling in long-range escort and ground-attack bombing, the aircraft was used by Australia, Brazil, France, the Soviet Union, and Great Britain—over 12,000 planes in all, more than any other U.S. fighter before or since.

Manufacturer: Republic Aviation Corporation **Type:** fighter **Engine:** Pratt & Whitney Double Wasp 18-cylinder radial air-cooled; P-47C—R-2800-21, 2,000 hp; P-47D—R-2800-59, 2,535 hp; P-47N—R-2800-57C, 2,800 hp **Dimensions:** wingspan P-47C/D—40 feet 9 inches, P-47N—42 feet 7 inches; length P-47B—35 feet 3.25 inches, P-47C/N—36 feet 1 inch, P-47D—36 feet 2 inches, P-47M—36 feet 4 inches; height P-47C/D—14 feet 2 inches, P-47N—14 feet 8 inches **Weight:** P-47B—13,360 pounds (loaded); P-47C—14,295 pounds (loaded); P-47D—19,400 pounds (loaded); P-47M—15,500 pounds (loaded); P-47N—20,500 pounds (loaded) **Speed:** P-47B—429 mph maximum; P-47C—433 mph maximum at 30,000 feet; P-47N—467 mph maximum at 32,500 feet, 300 mph cruise **Ceiling:** 42,000 feet **Range:** P-47B—1,250 miles with drop tank; P-47M—560 miles; P-47N—2,200 miles, with 2,000 pounds 800 miles **Armament:** 8 machine guns; P-47C—500 pounds of bombs; P-47D—2,500 pounds of bombs; P-47N—8 machine guns, 3,000 pounds of bombs **Crew:** 1

Photographs: pp. 30-31, p. 32, p. 33

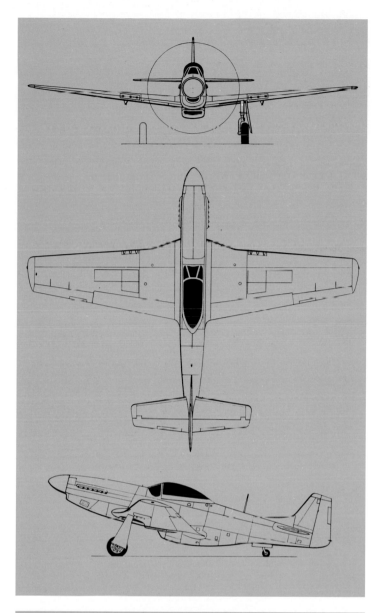

P-51 MUSTANG

When the British requested North American Aviation to build Curtiss P-40s under license for the RAF, company President J.H. "Dutch" Kindelberger countered with an offer to construct a superior aircraft using the same engine as the P-40, even though NAA had never before built a fighter. Within 117 days, the NA-73X prototype was completed, and in October 1940, it was airborne.

Designed to escort bombers over long distances, the P-51 combined every aerodynamic, structural, and systems advancement, resulting in exceptional internal fuel capacity and low drag. Drop tanks of 75 and 108 gallons were located under each wing, enabling the P-51 to reach every point in Western Europe.

In 1942 the aircraft's high-altitude limitation was overcome by using a 60-series Merlin engine. The P-51B version incorporated an intercooler radiator and augmented coolant and oil radiators and a large-area, four-blade propeller to absorb power at high altitudes.

The P-51 could out-perform the German Bf 109 or Fw 190 once its tanks were emptied and dropped. It became the leading U.S. fighter in Europe for the last 18 months of WWII.

Manufacturer: North American Aviation, Inc. **Type:** fighter **Engine:** 12-cylinder V liquid-cooled; P-51A—Allison V-1710-81, 1,200 hp; P-51B—Packard V-1650-3, 1,400 hp; P-51D—Packard V-1650-7, 1,510 hp; P-51H—Packard V-1650, 1,380 hp **Dimensions:** wingspan 37 feet; length P-51A/B/D—32 feet 3 inches, P51H—33 feet 4 inches; height P-51A—8 feet 8 inches, P-51B—12 feet 2 inches, P-51D/H—13 feet 8 inches **Weight:** P-51A—8,800 pounds (loaded); P-51B—11,200 pounds (loaded); P-51D—11,600 pounds (loaded) **Speed:** P-51A—390 mph maximum at 20,000 feet; P-51B—440 mph maximum at 30,000 feet; P-51C/D—437 mph maximum at 25,000 feet; P-51H—487 mph maximum at 25,000 feet, 380 mph cruise **Ceiling:** P-51A—31,350 feet; P-51B—42,000 feet; P-51D—41,900 feet **Range:** P-51A—750 miles; P-51B—810 miles; P-51D—950 miles; P-51H—2,400 miles, 850 miles with 1,000 pounds **Armament:** P-51A—4 machine guns, 1,000 pounds of bombs; P-51B—4 machine guns, 2,000 pounds of bombs; P-51D/H—6 machine guns, 2,000 pounds of bombs **Crew:** 1

Photographs: pp. 6-7, pp. 78-79, p. 80, p. 81, p. 82, p. 83, p. 86, pp. 86-87, pp. 88-89, pp. 110-111

P-61 BLACK WIDOW

The early successes achieved by the Royal Air Force radar-equipped night fighters prompted Northrop in 1940 to submit a design to meet the new needs of the U.S. Army Air Force. Their design focused on a heavy, high-winged, twin-engine aircraft that had tricycle landing gear and powerful engines. This design enabled the aircraft to carry a radar installation as well as powerful armament.

Northrop's proposal received enthusiastic support, and development began without delay. On May 21, 1942, the first prototype, the XP-61, flew. Problems with the air-borne radar equipment delayed completion, and it wasn't until early 1944 that the P-61A went into service.

Designated the Black Widow because of its black paint-scheme and its expected deadliness to the enemy, the P-61 was a three-seat night-fighter and bomber that demonstrated excellent overall performance, as well as lethal firepower from 1944 to 1952.

Manufacturer: Northrop Aircraft, Inc. **Type:** night fighter **Engine:** P-61B—two Pratt & Whitney R-2800-65 Double Wasp 18-cylinder radial air-cooled, 2,000 hp each **Dimensions:** wingspan 66 feet, length 49 feet 7 inches, height 14 feet 8 inches **Weight:** 38,000 pounds (loaded) **Speed:** 366 mph maximum at 20,000 feet, 235 mph cruise **Ceiling:** 33,100 feet **Range:** 3,000 miles (ferry), 1,050 miles (combat) **Armament:** 4 × 20mm cannon, 4 machine guns, 6,400 pounds of bombs **Crew:** 3

Photographs: pp. 40-41, p. 42, pp. 42-43, pp. 44-45

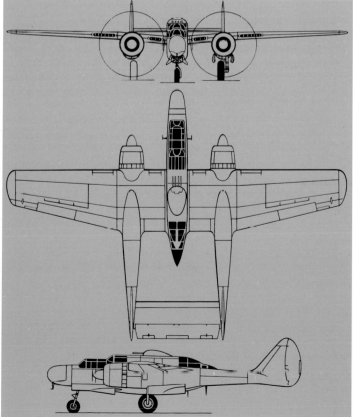

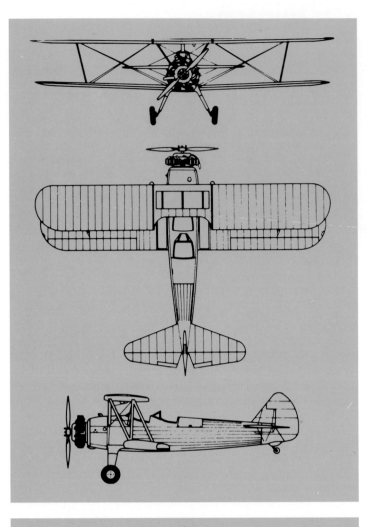

PT-17 KAYDET

Over 10,000 Boeing-Stearman Kaydets were produced between 1935 and 1945 for the U.S. Army Air Force and the U.S. Navy. A highly successful biplane, the PT Kaydet was based on an original Stearman design.

During that ten-year period, four variations were produced, each differing only in engines and equipment. There was a Lycoming engine in the PT-13, a Continental engine in the PT-17, and a Jacobs engine in the PT-18. The PT-27 was differentiated by its instrumentation and its enclosed cockpit design. It was manufactured for Canada.

All four versions of the Kaydet were among the most widely used basic trainers for the United States during WWII.

Manufacturer: Boeing Aircraft Company **Type:** trainer **Engine:** Continental, R-670-5 7-cylinder radial air-cooled, 220 hp **Dimensions:** wingspan 32 feet 2 inches, length 25 feet, height 9 feet 2 inches **Weight:** 2,717 pounds **Speed:** 124 mph maximum **Ceiling:** 11,200 feet **Range:** 505 miles **Armament:** none **Crew:** 2

Photographs: p. 46, p. 47

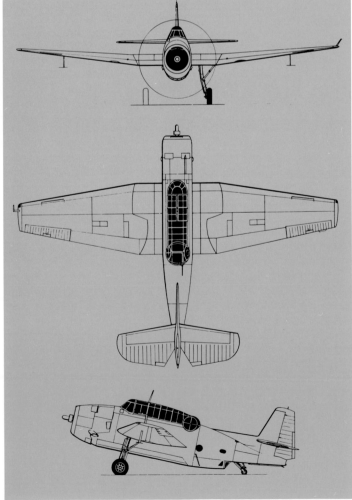

TBM AVENGER

Grumman Aircraft Engineering Corporation had never built an offensive aircraft before designing the replacement for the TBF-1 Avenger. The XTBF-1, which first flew in August 1940, was a sound machine with a tough airframe, wings with skewed hinges that allowed them to fold alongside the fuselage, an internal bay for torpedo or other ordnance, plenty of fuel, and a powered dorsal turret.

Eastern Aircraft was awarded a successive contract, delivering nearly identical models known as TBM in March 1942. Most of the Avengers produced were Eastern's TBM-3 model, noted for its powerful R-2600 engine, strengthened wings for increased gross weights, and reinforcement for carrying a radar scanner or rockets.

During the war, Eastern developed numerous, special-purpose TBM versions, used for photo-reconnaissance, transport, or night reconnaissance with early-warning equipment installed.

Other significant models were the 3E, which was the first specialized antisubmarine warfare aircraft to carry modern sensors and to operate from a carrier, and the 3W, which was the first aircraft to carry an early-warning radar in service.

Manufacturer: Eastern Aircraft Division of General Motors Corporation **Type:** torpedo bomber **Engine:** Wright 14-cylinder double-row Cyclone; TBM-1—R-2600-8, 1,700 hp; TBM-3—R-2600-20, 1,900 hp **Dimensions:** wingspan 54 feet 2 inches, length 40 feet **Weight:** TBM-3—18,250 pounds (loaded) **Speed:** 275 mph maximum **Ceiling:** TBM-1—22,400 feet; TBM-3—30,100 feet **Range:** 1,100 miles **Armament:** TBM-1—1 cannon; TBM-3—2 cannons **Crew:** 3

Photographs: pp. 134-135, p. 136, p. 137, pp. 140-141

The photographer gratefully acknowledges the assistance of the following individuals, whose gracious cooperation made this book possible: John Abramo, Vick Agather, John Alger, Ben Anderson, Neil Anderson, Bill Arnot, Bud Arnot, Tom Austin, Dick Baird, George Baker, Lynne Barber, John T Baugh, Dick Baughman, Dellon Baumgardner, Nelda Baumgardner, James Beasley, Bill Becker, John Bell II, Ralph Benhart, Bob Blankenship, Ruthie Blankenship, Dick Bodycombe, Hess Bomberger, Connie Bowlin, Ed Bowlin, Bob Byrne, Chris Campbell, Vince Carruth, Bill Carter, June Carter, Dick Caum, Mary Alice Caum, George Clark, William E. Clark, Glenn Coleman, Joe Coleman, Mike Collier, Bob Collings, Mike Collins, Buddy Cooksey, Bill Crump, Jay Cullum, Dean Cutshaw, Bill Dahlgren, Dick Daum, Don Davidson, Dick Deiter, Tom Deiter, John Dilley, Dennis Divine, Bill Dodds, Archie Donahue, Lyn Dowling, Pat Elliot, Bob Ellis, John Ellis, Joe Engle, Dick Ervin, Joan Ervin, Jeff Ethell, Susan Ewing, Dude Ezel, Nelson Ezel, Debbie Fetherston, Jennifer Fierro, Joe Frasca, Rudy Frasca, Lynn Gamma, Marvin L. Gardner, Ronnie Gardner, Bob Gear, Bill Godwin, John Goltra, Bill Greenwood, Wanda Gurr, Nelson Hall, Francis Hancock, H.M. Hancock, Roy Harris, Bill Harrison, John Hess, Tex Hill, Jack Hilliard, John Hinton, Steve Hinton, Jack Holden, Bill Holm, Christa Holm, Eddie Holmes, Jimmie Hunt, Charles Hutchins, David Karlson, John Kelley, Fred Kirk, Jim Kitchens, Bill Klaers, Dale Krebsbach, Sally Kyle, Kermit LaQuey, Kevin Larosa, Brenda Lofton, Harold Longberry, Howard Loveling, Jim Lowe, Joe Mabee, Ray Mabrey, Glen MacDonald, Leland L. Martin, Dan McCue, Danny McGee, Carter McGreggor, Jimmy McMillion, Pete McManus, Joe McShane III, Harry Merritt, Bob Mikesh, Madge Minton, Art Monig, Jack Moore, Julie Moore, Lloyd Nolen, Bill Northcut, Howard Pardue, Sue Parish, Pete Parish, Georgia Parish, Oz Parish, Ernie Persich, Walt Pine, Paul Poberezny, Tom Poppell, Sam Poss, Ed Pupek, Mike Pupich, Tom Reilly, Carol Reynolds, Ted Reynolds, Buck Ridley, Stephen Roberts, Chris Robinson, Gary Robinson, Peaches Robinson, Rick Ropke, Bill Ross, Ralph Royce, Scott Royce, Bill Russell, Jack Sadler, Rob Satterfield, Jaime Serra, Ari Silberman, John Silberman, Jack Skipper, Guy Joe Smith, John Souther, Bob Spaulding, Moon Spillers, George St George, Charles Stolenberg, Ann Strine, Russ Strine, Cory Stutzman, Ray Stutzman, Ray Thompson, Craig Timms, Walt Trainer, Joe Underwood, Richard Upstrom, R.L. Waltrip, Jack Webster, Pat Webster, Kermit Weeks, J.K. West, Jean Winkler, Arthur Wolk, Tom Wood, Walter Wooten, Jim Zazas, Tony Ziemiecki.

The publisher gratefully acknowledges the kind cooperation of Henry R. Beeson, Joseph S. Bochna, A. Hess Bomberger, Matt Carmack, Philip O. Carr, Archie Donahue, and David Lee "Tex" Hill.

With special thanks to F. Bradley Peyton III, for sharing his memories and personal materials, among them the diaries of Warren Hearn, Kirby H. Woehst, George M. Foote, and Herbert W. Gray, all members of the crew of "Tailwind," a B-24 Liberator of the 738th Squadron, 454th Bombardment Group (Heavy), 15th Army Air Force. Special thanks also to the press staff of Vice President George H. Bush for their assistance with his interview.